MEANDERINGS
WITH
Grace

GLIMPSES OF GOD IN
THE ORDINARY

RANDALL GEHRES

Wasteland Press
www.wastelandpress.net
Shelbyville, KY USA

Meanderings with Grace:
Glimpses of God in the Ordinary
by Randall Gehres

First Printing – October 2015
ISBN: 978-1-68111-063-9

Printed in the U.S.A.

0   1   2   3   4   5

ACKNOWLEDGEMENTS

Deepest thanks to:

Anna for her partnership in bringing this manuscript to publishing form, her editorial eye, computer savvy, and literary soul; and to Susannah for her insightful comments and prodding suggestions;

Pat and Earl for their encouragement and careful evaluation of the original material;

Dwaine for organizational advice;

Mark, Paul, and Eva for comments, shared experiences, and insights that found their way into this book;

Barbara, who first gave these *meanderings* their name;

Colleagues Elizabeth, Shirley, and Lisa for timely assistance;

Parishioners along the way with whom *meanderings* have become a dialogue of faith;

My wife, Grace, whose spirit is all over these pages.

TABLE OF CONTENTS

INTRODUCTION

ALMOST FIFTY YEARS HAVE PASSED SINCE I PUBLISHED ANYTHING. That was a poem in a youth magazine for which I received $25, about what I may net on this project. I might not have done this at all but for two people early on in the mountains of Tennessee, my first place of ministry after seminary.

John, a distinguished gentleman and respected educator, retired, said to me, "You ought to be a writer." We were not yet well acquainted. He had seen only a bit of my writing in church newsletters. He had heard from me more through sermons, a fact which did bring the thought that maybe he was suggesting a more likely career than preaching. But that is what he said, "You ought to be a writer." It stuck.

Doris was a parishioner turned friend who displayed an incredible amount of gumption in writing, painting, raising a family, and caring about her community while dealing from childhood with the serious effects of polio. She followed my ministerial journey from afar, encouraging me to keep writing, offering occasional critiques, at her death still urging me to publish these *Meanderings*. So, Doris, you win.

These writings have their roots in the Christian family into which I was born and the church in which I was raised. I met my wife, Grace, at college, we were married and a week later headed off to seminary. In more than one sense, *Meanderings with Grace* began then. I studied the theological doctrine of God's grace – free gift and undeserved gift that it is. But it was as a pastor that I began to see *grace* at work.

I have been a pastor almost forty years. There was also a bit of campus ministry, creating three Christian youth centers early on, and some community organizing with a mountain mission project. I served in student pastor roles in small town Massachusetts and suburban

Boston. But mostly I have been in three pastorates. First was the three-congregation ecumenical parish in the mountains of east Tennessee. Small in numbers, they had big hearts. They helped me understand what it means to be ordained to ministry, and how to be church when the institution is not flourishing. Second, a two-congregation pastorate in a six-church Larger Parish in the hills and Ohio River Valley of southeastern Ohio. They nurtured our young family, were full of holy spunk, and taught me how to be a pastor. Then we moved to a larger, downtown church in a small city of industry surrounded by farmland. For over twenty years now they have stretched me this way and that with their energy, creativity, and humor.

A young woman once said to me, "It doesn't sound like you believe in anything." She had come with her children to worship at our church a few times. I was trying to tell her about the church, but it was not working. She wanted to know who God is and what that had to do with her. She wanted to hear what I and my congregation knew and believed about God. Doctrine would not do; she wanted more than creeds. A few popular religious platitudes might have eased her pain, but I don't think so. "It doesn't sound like you believe in anything." What I was saying and how I was saying it were just not getting through.

Since that day, I have been trying to answer her and everyone else who wanders into the life of the church or inquires about Christian faith. What have I seen about God to believe in and trust? What do I glimpse of God in the ordinariness of life? Where have I noticed God at work when before I had not been paying attention? *MEANDERINGS WITH GRACE* is about those glimpses that lead to faith.

These reflections watch for where God becomes present to us in the most common happenings, where God shows up in the everyday. They wonder how we might trust the God we glimpse in those moments. They ask what it is to center our lives on this God best known in Jesus Christ. They endeavor to speak the faith in a different key.

My purpose in publishing is to express appreciation to parishioners for their companionship in meandering with me on faith's journey. It hopes to provide reflections for use in personal devotion or the church's life together. Most of all, it endeavors to offer seekers or any who simply wander by insight into the God of Christians whom we trust with our lives.

Transcending the differences of religious thought, faith practices, and spiritual sensibilities is the great human challenge of taking ourselves less seriously and God more seriously. I hope these *Meanderings with Grace* will help you along that way.

I AM NOT A WRITER

I WENT TO A WRITER'S CONFERENCE RECENTLY. There I learned that I am not a writer. It was kind of an expensive lesson, although the cookies were good. For one thing, I don't have an agent. Writers need an agent, so I learned (I am considering a professional sports agent who gets baseball players great contracts; I am not a baseball player, but then I'm not a writer either, so there you go). Writers are people with a craft, who work at it every day. For me, crafts topped out with gluing macaroni to plastic crosses in Bible School. Writers are driven; I peddle.

Besides, I am not nearly skilled enough on the computer to win an editor's favor. Getting the manuscript into the appropriate Word document form – double space, don't justify, New Times Roman, ham and cheese on rye but light on the *italics*, and don't double-double space between paragraphs or we'll have to institutionalize you. Only one space between sentences (see – I'm doing it all wrong). And get those spaces away from either end of the dash – dash it all. Who changed punctuation rules without asking me? Don't even get me started on syntax (which I think would be a wonderful way to raise revenue for the church).

Personal confession, but don't tell anybody: I don't even own a Chicago Style Guide for writing. There, I've said it. (Is that the one you fold in half to eat?) No, I am clearly not a writer.

Worse, I don't have a hook line for my writing. I learned this: you need a hook line to get a book published. What is a hook line? ("Hi there, do you come here often to read manuscripts"?) And what's with the fishing metaphors? Oh, and for heaven's sake, don't actually send the manuscript to an editor. Or email it. What they want to see is your hook line... and your platform. A platform turns out to be the number of people who know you and would be inspired to buy your book, since selling books seems to be of interest to editors. That takes care of that. No hook line, no platform, no craft – I'm not a writer.

What I do is get ideas about ordinary things which remind me of God, and I make some notes. Sometimes I think I see God lurking about, often in humorous ways, and I tell about it. Occasionally God jumps out of a burning bush in somebody's yard and surprises the heck out of me, and I jot it down so I won't forget. That's what I do.

I am jotting this down here because people often express to me that they don't think much of themselves as Christians. They can cite chapter and verse of their failures in Christian living. They consider themselves weak in the following of Jesus. I usually agree. They are right. But that's not the point.

God takes the lives we are writing and makes something good out of them. God takes our discipleship with all its shortcomings and syntax and the things we have wrongly *italicized* and blesses them into something that God can use. We are God's platform, invited to not only pick up God's best-selling Book, but also to watch for the sequel in which we are major characters.

PART ONE:

God

SPINNING

FIGURE SKATERS WIN STYLE POINTS DOING THIS ON SKATES. I did it in a car.

I turned onto a nice, flat piece of road on a snowy day where the snow had been cleared away so that I confidently began to accelerate. The next thing I knew was my vehicle beyond my influence and control, as I went round and round in a circle right there in the middle of the road. Fortunately, this bit of road broadened into four lanes wide, and there was no traffic near me as I spun my dangerous dance.

Inside the car I could only hold on as the world circled dizzily around me. I knew that out there were houses, hills, a bridge, and the Ohio River, but all I could see was a rotating blur peppered with snowflakes.

Love is like this, if you've ever fallen into it. It spins you around and around in a giddy blur. Even when reality slows down the spinning, love continues to leave you crazily out of control. Suffering and sorrow are like this as well, spinning you into a dark and dangerous place where the brakes are not effective and you cannot get what is happening to you to stop.

God's love in Jesus Christ is like this. God's love comes into the world in a physical and tangible way in the person of Jesus. God's love then invites us in, sits us down, and begins to whirl us around like my car on ice until the world as we knew it is only a blur. It is still out there, our old and familiar world. But sitting in the midst of God's love changes what we see.

What we see is Jesus, the walking and talking love of God, who is afflicted and agonized.

God draws us into Jesus' suffering and sorrow, spins us around in it, until we come to see how it changes us, frees us, cleans us, transforms and reinvigorates our lives as if we have just been raised from the dead. The blurry, groaning world around us is likewise being spun into something new and resurrected.

God's love may not be like a placid mountain lake after all, but a car spinning out of my control and into God's.

WRONG BURNER

I HAD BEEN ON THE PHONE ALL MORNING, one call after another for the past three hours. Hungry, I decided to make a toasted cheese sandwich. So I brought out the iron skillet, turned on the stove burner to warm the skillet, and began to prepare the sandwich. The phone rang again. When it became clear that the call would involve some time, I turned off the burner and moved the skillet to a cool back burner.

After a while, I decided that I could continue this phone business and fix my sandwich at the same time, so I turned the burner back on, completed the sandwich, and placed it in the skillet. The warm skillet was soon melting the butter against the iron. Good cook that I am, and not wanting a burnt sandwich, I knew this would take my keen attention and utmost concentration. After a few moments, I examined the sandwich, but the cheese was not melted, nor was the bread turning a toasty brown.

I turned up the heat. After a proper interval, another examination revealed no further browning. So I turned up the heat some more. Time passed. I checked again – no toasted cheese, just buttery warm bread. I turned it up yet again. You see, I've been to college, and I know that higher heat will have an effect. When yet another investigation showed no change in my sandwich, it occurred to me that something was not quite right here. I am very quick on the uptake about such things. With the sandwich languishing in an only warm skillet, I noticed heat emanating from the vacant front burner.

And I began to form the notion that the skillet might be on the wrong burner. I was trying to make a toasted cheese sandwich on a by-now-mostly-cold burner. The skillet was only in the neighborhood of the heat. It reflects favorably on my cooking prowess that I quickly rectified the situation.

But it did give pause. What else in my life is on the wrong burner? Or yours, what in your life rests on a burner that cannot fulfill its promise? What in your life is supposed to be soon sizzling, but actually sits on a cold burner? Have you put your faith in something once seemingly hot but now grown cold?

Christian faith knows that the dependable foundation, the true rock, the reliable cornerstone is Jesus the Christ. Christ is the burner that is always cooking. Christ is the burner that never grows cold. Christ is the burner that is always working to transform your life into something good.

Have you been trusting in the wrong burner?

WONDERFULLY MADE

A RED TULIP THAT IS JUST ABOUT TO OPEN, swaying gently in the sunshine, is quite incredible. Seven such tulips bunched together are too much; the intricate wonder of a single tulip blends into a blaze of color. Better to look at just one. How does God do that? Such workmanship! Did the Creator make any mistakes?

An old movie had God admitting to an error with avocados, having made the pit too big. Many would beg to differ, convinced that the popular avocado is fine the way it is, thank you very much. How about ostriches, asked the movie, didn't something go wrong in the creating of these odd creatures?

How about that telemarketer whose phone call interrupted my amazement at the tulip, and then hung up on me, did the Creator make him on a Friday? Or people who can find no other answer to problems and fears except violence: did the Creator mix the wrong ingredients with them?

How about you – did the Creator make any mistakes with you? Pit too big? Legs too long?

John Calvin (of great theologian fame) said that God could have created us for usefulness, but instead created us **for God's sheer delight.** Each one of us is made, fashioned, and formed for the delight of God. I am pretty sure it was the Creator's sense of humor that was delighted in the making of me. Can you consider that you have been created, intentionally unique in your own way from all others, for God's sheer delight? That you are a delight in the eyes of your Maker?

How are you feeling about yourself and the life you have? I'm sure God is not pleased with some of the things you have to put up with, nor with some of the things you have done. And yet there is something about you. Of all creatures, *you* have been created to be delightful to God.

Standing there in the sunshine apart from the crowd, you are that tulip, incredibly made, for the joy of your Creator.

LOVE

ACROSS THE ROOM OF THIS COFFEE SHOP sits a young mother with her infant son. The boy is just old enough to be held upright without his head bobbing. Awake now from a nap, he is held by his mother with such tender love, honored with gentle kisses, that it almost takes my breath away. He is enveloped in the aura of love's safety, security, trust and goodness, love's well-being – fed, rested, properly diapered.

His adoring grandmother reaches for him. She coaxes without embarrassment. She wants the child to come to her that she might hold him. But he is not interested in an adventure. He is fine in his mother's love. Eventually another young woman, probably his aunt, grabs and holds him, trying to communicate with strange sounds and movements. Then the grandmother gets her wish, and the boy is off to another pair of arms and a new voice, touch, and smell. He is OK with this adventure that has sought him out, but is glad (and, am I imagining, *relieved*) to return to his mother, into her care and closeness and love.

On the Sundays after Easter, our talk in the church turns to God's love. Having been impressed once again with the power of God that brings resurrection and new life in so many ways, we now take a new look at the love behind that power. We reflect on God's self-giving love poured out for us. We see Christ as the Good Shepherd who so loves his sheep that not one of them should be lost. We hear how we abide in this love as a vine is connected to its branches, and how we are to bear love's fruit. We welcome the promise that God's love forgives, strengthens, persists, and will not let us go.

I do not pretend to comprehend the width and height and depth of God's love for me. Or even why God would offer it to me. But if it is anything like the infant held in his mother's love so tender, so complete

and unstinting, cradled in such happiness and goodness and well-being
– tummy full and diaper clean – it is alright with me.

MEMORY

ON THE LAST DAY OF CHURCH CAMP, as the campers were preparing to depart, one camper put his hands on the shoulders of Kevin his counselor and said with feeling, "I will never forget you, David."

David?

It has become commonplace for sportscasters to comment on some acclaimed sports figure as one "who will forever be remembered… "

Forever?

The shingles on our church roof have been there about 10 years but have a *lifetime guarantee*. Lifetime? Whose: The seller's lifetime, the property committee's lifetime, the building's lifetime, mine, yours? And who will be around to recall that guarantee when it is needed?

I find it humbling to look at a grave marker that is still standing tall but the name once clearly etched is now worn so as to be unreadable. Forever remembered? Heroes are buried to the tune of fierce vows that they will never be forgotten. But of course eventually they are. Even those most beloved to us, once in death can slip away from vivid memory, not all at once, or completely, but nevertheless.

Given this, I find God's memory comforting. Though the world's memory is necessarily limited, God says, "*Fear not… I have called you by name. You are mine.*"[1] You will not be forgotten. You will become part of God's long memory. Even better: who you are after death will be one who lives in God's presence and love. This is God putting a hand on your shoulder and promising, "I will never forget you."

In this is our lifetime guarantee, God's memory is the great forever.

---

[1] Isaiah 43:1

KEYS

THE OTHER DAY, I THREW MY KEYS INTO THE TRASH CAN. I did not mean to. Having pulled the ring of keys from the car ignition, I grabbed a handful of old paper, tissues, and sandwich wrappers from the car to discard. Laden with bags and other items to be carried inside, I dropped the handful of trash into the bin, including, apparently, my keys. Keys: car, house, church, the whole ring.

I say *apparently* because it was not until later, having searched everywhere, that it occurred to me for some reason to check the trash can. I continue to break new ground in mindless action.

But that is not news.

What is good news is that God has not given to me the keys of the kingdom. Well, I know that scripture says Jesus gave to Peter the keys to the kingdom of heaven, which we have interpreted to mean given to the church in general.[2] The church by its faithful witness and ability to speak and live the Gospel holds the keys for others to know and enter into God's everlasting love. But we do not get to be the gatekeeper deciding for whom to unlock heaven's doors, or not.

That should be a great relief. Can you imagine the best of us – with our resentments and prejudices, likes and dislikes, our retaliatory instincts, and sense of people getting what they deserve – holding the keys to the kingdom? Heaven would be considerably less populated.

Worse, can you imagine, well, *me* in charge of the keys? "Just a minute, I know they are here somewhere. Now where did I put them? Did you notice if the trash hauler came by yet? I know you want in. Please be patient, even if it does seem to be taking an eternity."

---

[2] Matthew 16:19

The Good News is that God, through the death and resurrection of Jesus Christ, has opened the gates. The Word is that the future is in God's hands, that Christ is the key and God is the judge, and that the judgment is God's love. At the cross, God's love is poured out, and the verdict is grace. Grace: a free gift from God, altogether at God's discretion. You are completely in God's hands on this one – body and soul, in life and in death. And that is a good thing. It is a comforting thought.

Less comforting: that you or I somehow hold the keys. In which case, I hope God has kept a spare.

HUMMINGBIRD

MY WIFE HEARD SOUNDS OF DISTRESS coming from a crack in the ground. Investigating, she found in that crack a trapped hummingbird. A sidewalk ran alongside the front of the brick parsonage where we were living. The years and the winters had caused that sidewalk to pull away from the foundation of the house, leaving a crack wide enough for a hummingbird to fall in and become lodged. Most likely the hummingbird flew into the window pane and, stunned, dropped into that crack just below. Unfortunately, not only was the tiny bird stuck there, but the crack was so deep and the bird so far down that it was hard to see how it could be rescued.

There was however a man working nearby on a project at the church. Consulted about the situation, he came over to the house, knelt down for a closer look, then called for a wire clothes hanger. Bending and twisting that hanger around, he was somehow able to manipulate it beneath the hummingbird and gently inch it up and out. It seemed both simple and miraculous. The hummingbird flew away.

I have in mind that image of man and hummingbird. How often have I learned from you or discovered for myself how we get ourselves lodged and stuck in the most impossible dilemmas. How frightening and discouraging it can be. How hopeless the prospect of redeeming the situation. How humbling to realize our helplessness and need for rescue beyond what we can see or manage. How like a fragile hummingbird in a deep crack in the ground.

Yet, there is God bending over us. One whom we did not expect to see in human form is bending down, bending heaven and earth to save us. There is God personally taking on the job of setting us free and restoring us to life. There is God in workman's overalls and a carpenter's cap bending down as if the only thing in the world that mattered in that moment is us.

EITHER WAY

As the hospital patient noted that all the tubes and needles were now unhooked and unplugged, I responded encouragingly, "That means you probably won't be around much longer." I probably could have phrased that better.

I meant, of course that the patient was surely on schedule to soon return home. Then again, the seeker of clarity might ask, which home – my home on Oak Street or the Big Home in the Sky?

The answer which Christians trust and proclaim is, "It doesn't matter!" It does not matter whether it is your earthly home or heavenly home to which you are headed next week, or what it means that you "probably won't be around much longer." Well, it does matter in the short run. It would be great to go home to one's family, to take that vacation this summer, to worship again at church on Easter, to complete that project, finish reading that trilogy, and see the Tribe finally win a World Series, to go on enjoying God's gift of life on this earth.

But in the long run it does not matter how much longer we will be around here, because Christ has died and Christ is risen. Now therefore, *whether we live or whether we die, we belong to Christ, who is Lord of both the dead and the living.*[3] I confess to not understanding exactly what that means. But in a way we can only guess, these words matter eternally. Somehow, Christ's own death and resurrection telescope our own life and death until they amount to the same thing – we belong to Christ.

Whether I live or die, I am under Christ's authority and care. That is the joy undergirding Christian faith and the assurance behind a Christian funeral. So when someone says "you won't be around here

---

[3] Romans 14

much longer," take it as Good News. Yes, your life today matters, is beloved, precious. But that will not change with death, for in Christ you matter eternally, precious to God, forever beloved.

TOGETHERNESS

THERE IS WITHIN OUR CHURCH FAMILY a couple who have been married for 68 years. That in itself is remarkable and worthy of salute. Such examples of marriages that prosper and endure are important models and encouragement for the rest of us. Blessings on all those who have achieved that and more! There is more. During those 68 years, not one day passed without this couple spending some time together. Yikes! Not one day apart: That is (by my longhand multiplication) 24,820 days plus about 17 leap days. Together. Every day. Think about it.

It is said that "absence makes the heart grow fonder." Apparently not. They have been together for 24,820 + 17 days in a row and counting, and appear all the better for it. I am not making this up. Still, there must have been some days, a few cranky and difficult days, when the thought of a day off must have looked attractive. (Why didn't he take the hint when I bought him that "Trip for One" to the North Pole?)

Would I surprise you to mention that in the Bible God is described as our marriage partner? That seems to be how God sees it, a marriage relationship with God's people. Promises have been made, faithfulness vowed, and we are supposed to be there for each other. Every day, year after year. Why is it then that God so often talks like an affronted spouse, not so much mistreated as ignored and feeling abandoned? *Where did you go? Why didn't you call? Why couldn't I go with you? Why didn't you come back?* We have things to do, and places to go. What does God expect: *every* day?

Is that what it means to be Jesus? Jesus is God's way of being with us, walking among us, talking with us, every day. Jesus is God's love drawing close to us and touching us daily. Jesus is the physical evidence of God's commitment to us.

Sometimes it is hard for us to believe certain things about God, things we think or are told we are supposed to believe, doctrines about who God is and how God works. What if the faith question is turned from *belief* to *trust*? Instead of "do you believe such-and-such about God," answer this question: *"do you trust God to be with you?"* Day after day, year after year, no matter what, do you trust that God will be with you -- 24,820 days in a row and forever?

BUCKEYE TREE

DURING THE TIME BEFORE WE WERE MARRIED, I gave my wife a buckeye tree for a birthday present. This was a somewhat more romantic gift than the garden hoe a few years later.

Much later still, I came to understand that she actually appreciated jewelry – who knew?

This buckeye tree was a sapling I dug up from along the creek back home. She planted it in a likely place for growth, an uncultivated area near woods and water. It struggled. Walkers were hard on it. A brush hog came through. A horse's shoe laid it low. It survived somehow, a dead stick in the ground with the faintest showing of a bud along the stem. Mesh wire was placed around this foot high tree to mark and protect. But it hardly grew.

Finally the tiny stick-of-tree was transplanted to a new location amid weeds and large rocks. It thrived. Now decades later that sapling is a boisterous buckeye tree which shades the area and annually covers the ground with an offering of new buckeye seeds.

Isn't this how God works? We labor and plan, plant and scheme, utilize feasibility studies and long range forecasts, and otherwise do our best, often with little or poor results. Then God breathes life into the idea, blesses the stick, and causes it to flourish in surprising places and ways.

This is certainly the story of ministry, as I can testify. It strikes me as the experience of the church, for those who have eyes to see. This working of God is what we know of the *kingdom of God* in which the future where God's will is done breaks wonderfully into our present moment. What is broken down shoots up again, the almost dead hope springs to life, and the meek inherit the earth. It has nothing to do with us and everything to do with us. Just a stick in the ground in our hands, now, by the grace of God, has become the tree of life.

UNDERSERVED

DOGGONE, IT'S COLD. Maybe not where you are reading this or if it is summer, but right now where I am it is cold. I cannot help but muse, "What did we do to deserve this?"

The question of getting what we deserve is persistent and powerful. The thought of it justifies capital punishment, giving that "low-life" what he deserves. It motivates theft and cheating, "I deserve what everyone else has." It rationalizes abuse, "I must have deserved that beating." It sometimes surprises us with ingratitude, "No, I cannot accept that; I don't deserve it."

A sustained reading of the Gospel of Luke may upset you or may set you free, I don't know which, for Luke reports that Jesus does not give a hoot about what you deserve. To put it more pointedly, Jesus knows full well that you deserve to be taken to the woodshed, but he brings you a load of firewood instead. (It's cold, remember?) Jesus knows you do not deserve any special consideration, but he brings you a bagful of gifts, and it is everything you really need. You don't deserve it. It is called *grace*.

The grace of God: *grace* means you don't deserve it, but you get it anyway because that's the way God wants it. You may not deserve love, but God loves you. You may not deserve forgiveness, but there it is 70 times 7. You may not deserve a second chance, but God offers a thirty-second. You may not deserve mercy, but mercy pours out. You find yourself in it knee-deep wherever you roam, the undeserved grace of God.

I still do not think we deserve this weather. Thank heaven we do not get what we deserve.

COMFORT

I DO LIKE TO BE COMFORTABLE. This is especially true if the alternative is discomfort. Others seem to have picked up on this. They regularly offer to provide me with a comfortable mattress, comfort recliner, comfortable shoes, a comfortable vacation spot or cruise for relaxing. As to the cost, the providers say that I deserve the comfort whatever the price. Actually, I'm all for it whether I deserve it or not.

Then there is the comfort of having a good job, of a home where you belong, and of knowing that somebody loves you. It is a comfort to start a journey with a full tank, to have the prayers and support of friends in a difficult time, and to know that your political party is in power. It may be to you a comfort in the middle of a hard week to anticipate that come Friday night your favorite show is on TV.

Some are so concerned with my comfort that they telephone me about security systems to wear around my neck or install in my house. They say that this would give me reassuring comfort, and maybe it would. Pre-arranged funerals are also a great comfort, I am told. I can see how that may be, just as long as they don't want to schedule it yet.

I am surprised to note how much of my life has to do with comfort: Are you comfortable to be a liturgist and speak in front of a crowd? Are you comfortable with the wedding service as planned? Are you comfortable in that hospital bed or would you like another pillow to support your neck? Are you comfortable that we can meet this budget? Are you comfortable with our rehearsal of this music? Are you comfortable with your daughter going off to that college?

Into this world of comfort comes Jesus with a message: ***your only comfort is that you belong to God.*** He says as much in the Beatitudes, in his Prodigal Son parable, in healing the centurion's son, in demonstrating God's love poured out for us. Not that God's comfort is a shade superior alongside other comforts, but that it is the only true comfort.

The very first question of the Heidelberg catechism asks, *"What is your only comfort in life and in death?"* In life and in death. And the answer, *"That I belong, body and soul in life and in death, not to myself but to my faithful Savior Jesus Christ."*[4] You belong – body and soul – to God. That is your only comfort, when it comes down to it. Some do not seem to find the idea of "belonging to God" comforting or good news.

I find it to be the best news we could ever be given.

---

[4] Heidelberg Catechism: a teaching tool summarizing Christian faith

NAMED

LAST NIGHT I RECEIVED A PHONE CALL from someone in California looking for Randall Gehres. But I was not the one he was trying to find. I always sort of figured that I am the only one around with this name. Now it turns out that there is another, maybe more of us. As if the world did not have enough problems.

A name identifies us, and helps others to know who we are. A teacher with a new class gets to know the students by name. The name differentiates us. It also connects us. If the teacher had your older brother with the same last name in class, she thinks she already knows something about you. Then again, if there have been 12 with the name of Peter Gehres in the village of Breitenheim, Germany, it is hard to know which ones belong to your family tree.

A name may get to be popular: in 2012, *Grace* ranked 12th in newborn names. Or not: *Randall* ranked 859th.

Do you ever wonder how God keeps track of us all? Psalm 139 indicates that God knows each of us personally as a unique creation: *O Lord, you have searched me and known me. You know when I sit down… you discern my thoughts… you knit me together in my mother's womb… I am fearfully and wonderfully made.* Moreover, Isaiah 43 states that God knows us by name: *Thus says the Lord, he who created you… "I have called you **by name**, you are mine."*

I am very impressed by that, honored, and somehow encouraged. Aren't you?

Though I am not particularly good at names, I like it when someone remembers mine. It is good to be known. It is good to be known by God, singled out of all the people in the world. It is good to be known by name.

Still, it must be quite a job. I wonder if God uses *name association,* "Let's see, RG... Radically Gifted, no... Reliably Grateful, no... Really Goofy, hmmm..."

DEBT

THE RESTAURANT BILL CAME TO $838.23. For the four of us. It was a celebratory meal at a local, modestly priced eatery. The bill came to me, $38.23. I handed over my credit card to the server at my table. She didn't come back. Twenty minutes went by and no sign of her. There was quite a pile-up of people near the door as some were trying to pay at the counter or perhaps find out the reason for the delay.

I was the reason. Or, rather, my bill was the reason. The person "taking care of us" had just charged my credit card $800 too much. $838.23. Endeavoring to rectify the situation, she then charged me an additional $838.23. Now I was into this meal for some $1,600. Plus tip. By the time I sauntered up to the counter, the crowd there had dispersed, and our server was scurrying about taking care of other tables, probably trying to decide how to break the news to me. After a while she came back, told me what had happened, and again took up trying to undo the financial tangle. Lest the $1600 charge balloon higher, I offered to pay cash for the $38.23 bill, thinking I could cancel the credit card charges later. She generously said, "No, because of the confusion and wait, there would be no charge at all."

The manager however either did not get that message or else had a different point of view. In the end, my credit card showed no charges for $838.23. But there was one for $38.23, the original cost of the meal. That was fair. Possibly it was not the best public relations, but fair. I paid for what I owed.

Those with a bookkeeping turn of soul like to note how we run up a debt with God. They are thinking about what we call *sins* – our disobedience to God's commands and betrayal of the Creator's purpose for our lives – "We have done those things we ought not to have done, and left undone those things we ought to have done." We run up quite a debt, more than we can pay off by trying to make amends, the debt growing faster than we can put things right again. An impossibly high debt. Lord, have mercy.

And that is exactly what happens. God has mercy. The outcome of our tangle of spiritual debt to God is zero debt. "There will be no charge." It turns out that God is not much of an accountant. God doesn't keep a ledger on us. Or maybe it is that God came to us in Christ to straighten out the books, and when Christ was finished there was no debt left on our balance sheet. Still isn't.

I ended up paying the restaurant what I properly owed. That seems only right. Many of us may think we would prefer such a business relationship with the Lord, certain that we could pay our own way and keep up with the payments.

God does not work that way – pay as you go, as if we could – but rather **grace**, **grace**, grace.

NO PROBLEM

SO I AM WALKING WITH ARMS FULL of this and that out of a store, and a young man holds the door for me. "Thank you," I say. "No problem," he responds. At the conclusion of a restaurant meal, I comment to the server, "This was a great meal; I appreciate your service." She replies, "No problem." After an older man gives me directions for getting to where I want to go, I offer my thanks and gratitude. His rejoinder: "No problem."

Apparently, *"No Problem"* is becoming the new *"You are welcome"*. Being a creature of culture, this new response does not seem to be quite right to me. *"You are welcome"* indicates that a courtesy or kindness was involved. *You are welcome* to my service, my act of courtesy, my kindness. It suggests that a most basic human respect is present. I give of myself to you, even if in the smallest of ways.

"No problem" seems to change the whole thing into a problem that does not exist. No problem – you got out the door, through your meal, where you were going. Nothing meaningful happened. No problem. Humility may be intended, but it denies that courtesy or a small act of compassion occurred. It was nothing. (People also say that sometimes.)

God does not say that to us. At worship or prayer, offering our thanks to God, the reply is not *"no problem"*. The Lord does not shrug it off. We owe God thanks for good reason. There is a problem. *We* are a problem, and there is no denying it. Our sin is a problem. Our disobedience that separates us from God so that we can hardly find our way back – problem. Our turning away from God to our own ways – that is a problem. It is real.

34

So was Jesus. His suffering was a problem. The cross was a real problem. Jesus' death was a problem.

When we say to the Lord, "Thank you," the reply is not, "no problem." but rather the response of scarred hands and open arms: "You are – *welcome.*"

SMART PHONE

I AM TALKING WITH MY MOTHER ON THE PHONE. It is Sunday afternoon, time for far-flung members of the family to catch up with one another. So my mother and I are having a good, long chat.

It occurs to me as we speak that it is getting about time to watch for a text message from my son in London. He is going to inform me about when exactly this afternoon he wants to Skype. So I go for my cell phone. Not on my desk. Where did I leave it? Not in my jeans pocket. Is it upstairs on the dresser? I am, you understand, continuing to converse with my mother as I search for that cell phone. No, it is not on the dresser. Suit pocket: no. Did I leave it in the basement? Not that I can see. Maybe it is in the van…

Wait. I am talking on it now. It's in my hand. It is the phone I have been using! I have been holding it for the last half hour.

My mother, when I told her, found this to be hilarious. Please don't inform my brother.

It is good that there is only one way to communicate with God – talk. Just talk, whether such praying is from your head or heart or mouth. Talk to God; you do not need a device.

God may at times seem to be far off, absent even. You search, trying to find God, "seeking the Lord while he may be found," when – *wait* – God is near, right at hand after all, all along.

Right at hand: Smart phone? Smart God.

WEED WHACKING

It was so simple. But I couldn't see it. For my weed whacker, I purchased a new head which holds the string that whacks off the weeds. New as of last summer, the unusual design promised to work better than the old kind. And so it did, until the string ran out, and the head needed to be restrung. I could not figure it out. Just wrap the string around... but how? I had not looked at it for almost a year. Just how does one begin? No directions were included, of course, since this was so simple.

Groucho Marx once commented, "This (device) is so simple a four-year-old child could understand it. Run out and find me a four-year-old child." That's what I did – not a four-year-old but young enough to be a third of my age. The young man held the gizmo in a puzzled way that told me he did not know how this one worked either. And I was gratified to see that he had to study on it all of 10 seconds before he solved it.

It really was simple. I just couldn't see it.

Karl Barth, the great twentieth century Reformed theologian, wrote many massive and profound tomes about God and the centrality of Christ and its meaning for the Church. Barth's writings have kept many a theological faculty busy trying to wrap themselves around his insights and obscurities. But when asked for a summary statement of what he believed, Barth said, "Jesus loves me, this I know, for the Bible tells me so."

If that young man who put me back to work weed whacking ever came to me with questions of faith – deep and complicated questions concerning the nature of God and the mystery of Christ and the hopes of eternity, obviously full of doubt and misgiving, seeking understanding

– I hope that I would ponder no more than 10 seconds before responding, "Jesus loves you, this I know."

STARING

"I WISH THAT I COULD PRAY the way my dog stares at the dinner table," Martin Luther once commented. Would that we could communicate with God with such single-minded longing! Our dog has his own soulful stare that he casts toward us through the outside window, willing us to come outside or to let him inside so that we can be together.

Our cat, however, uses "the stare" more effectively. When she wants human companionship, she will sit and stare at one of us until that person sits or lies down on the floor. Then she curls up on the proffered lap or back or legs and falls asleep. It is a powerful stare. She has been known to stare at the back of a child who is practicing the piano until that child is compelled to cease practicing and get down on the carpet instead.

I wonder if God works that way with us. When God's love finds no traction, longing for us without response, when we blithely go along our way unheeding any word from the Lord, does God just stare at us until we notice and obey?

Do you ever sense God staring at you?

PART TWO:

Spiritual Life

ALLIGATORS

My wife commented, "What happens if there is an alligator on the path?" We were in a wildlife refuge, walking along a raised pathway that divided the swamp. Trees and brush lined the path giving it a shadowy and slightly unsettling effect. Especially since we were counting the alligators, large and small, just yards away down the bank in the brackish water or sunning themselves with one eye seemingly measuring us. Eight alligators, nine, ten… We were retracing our steps from a hike to a lake on the only path (as far as we knew) that would return us to the visitor's center and our car. To the right and the left: 18 gators, 19, 20.

"So what do we do if an alligator is on the path?" she asked, causing us to look up and down the path ahead. Sure enough, about 50 yards ahead, there stood an eight-foot gator straddling the path, blocking it completely. That gave us pause. Our way lay ahead. But the alligator was not budging. Now what? Should I arm myself with a stick? Send my wife ahead to shoo away that gator? Wait, and hope the other reptiles stay put?

The Christian life is a journey of faith, we are told. Walk in trust and obedience, following the Jesus way, a path straight and narrow. It is the way of life, we are promised. But what about the alligators that cross the path and stand in the way? There are always alligators. Illness, unemployment, doubt, anxiety, fear, genuine evil, you have seen them. Alligators on the Christian path, they block the way.

"Let not your hearts be troubled," Jesus said about these gators. Nothing can block us from the love of God in Christ Jesus. After all, Jesus is Lord. This is the conclusion of Easter. The risen Christ is Lord, ascended to rule heaven and earth; even the alligators must submit. Sooner or later, they will crawl off and away, leaving only the blessed path of the glory of God. In the meantime, God gives us the *Spirit* to go with us on the way, to be our Companion on the path, our Comforter against the gators, our Guide home. Don't be afraid. God is with us.

Back on that path through the swamp, the alligator eventually moved on to where it belonged. What path are you on?

BORING

ON THE ROAD IN FRONT OF OUR HOUSE was painted in large white letters, **#10 BORE**, with an arrow pointing to where I lived. Some assured me that this had to do with the laying of new water pipelines. Maybe so, but there was another possibility: on a scale of 1 to 10, with #10 being the ultimate level of boring, the pastor to which this arrow pointed... Well, do I need to say it?

But let's talk about us. On a scale of 1 to 10, how boring are we together? Again, that can be read in one of two ways. Are we as a church, you know, boring? Are we unexciting, causing others to grow weary, ourselves dissatisfied? Or, are we *boring* as in digging into something, moving ahead steadily, and exploring important depths? Is our church *boring* down deep into the life of faith?

I am not sure that a church is supposed to be entertaining. We are not here to be measured against the entertainment industry or show biz religion. But the church does carry the word of life. You can recognize life in the church when you see it, the living Christ present there. Are we boring? Are we digging into the Scriptures, drilling toward God in prayer, inching forward in Christian service?

Spiritually, we can never stay put. Either we are becoming less excited and less exciting with the Gospel, and therefore more boring, or we are persistently and adventurously boring into the deep riches of living by faith in the God we know through Jesus. Isn't this true individually as well? Has your spiritual life leveled off, cooled off, found a resting place with God that seemed good enough, and thereby is slipping into boring? Or are you faithfully boring into new layers of forgiveness, untapped depths of love, and yet to be explored trust in God?

If the arrow on the road in front of your house were pointing to *you*, which "boring" would it signify?

WATER SLIDE

I did not expect the thrills to be quite so public. Some in my family were at a water park where waterslides offer a revelation of fun. Now it is true that those great slides of water ridden on a raft take your breath away. But they leave your clothes intact. Since the waiting lines were so long for those breathless rides, we decided to try the *body slides*. Starting high above the ground, flat on your back and feet first, you speed downward on the flowing water in an enclosed tube, around curves and sometimes a bit airborne, finally splashing into a pool. I figured I could do that (if kids less than a quarter of my age could). I did. Down I went, whispering "What am I doing here?" Despite the bumping on my back and side (read "backside"), it was a thrill.

I struggled up out of the pool of water to get into line again when I noticed a bit of a draft. A quick glance showed that the slide had ripped my swimsuit. Closer examination increasingly revealed, well, the side and back of the swimsuit had been ripped to shreds. This, you understand, is the swimsuit I was wearing – if you can call it that. Fortunately, there were no more than hundreds of people all around me. Unfortunately, my towel was about a hundred yards away, in the midst of a teeming crowd of families of young children. Through this crowd, with one hand at hip trying to hold the shreds together, I now proceeded to stroll, sporting the waddle of an affected swimsuit model.

My family found this to be quite enjoyable, even more so when I eventually reappeared in the only replacement swimsuit I could buy at the water park, a size too small and psychedelic Hawaiian.

"Rejoice in the Lord always," wrote the Apostle Paul to followers of Christ. I assume he meant **always**, in all circumstances, including water sliding and its repercussions. He also added, *"Do not worry about*

anything... let your gentleness be known to everyone."[5] I don't know about my gentleness, but much became known.

Rejoice in the Lord always. I like the sound of that, but find it far easier said than done. Joy is more often known as one area of life occasionally visited, but mostly hoped for. Nevertheless, this is Paul's clear-sighted Gospel: **Joy is the birthright of Christians.** Rejoice in the Lord always, in all things.

Don't hold back. Rejoice! Or, as Paul might have said of that day at the water park: when confronted with challenges and burdens, put to the test by others, and striving to live faith boldly, *let 'er rip*!

---

[5] Philippians 4:4-7

WEDDING DRESS

To find a proper wedding dress for the mother of the groom turns out to be a big deal. So when that was satisfactorily accomplished, my wife was not the only one to let out a sigh of relief. A new pair of extremely comfortable yet appropriately dressy sandals was a happy bonus. So far, so good.

On the morning of the wedding, the mother of the groom and I dressed in our wedding attire, then on the way to the festivities we stopped at a supermarket to pick up two previously ordered fruit trays. These fruit trays were marvelous to behold. Not just a single layer, there were mounds of fruit stacked upon each other many inches deep – melon of various kinds, pineapple, grapes, strawberries, blueberries, but particularly watermelon which seemed to be the juicy theme that held it all together.

Having sent me on an errand elsewhere in the store, my wife headed for the deli section where a woman placed the two plastic-covered fruit trays, one atop the other, on the high deli shelf. The top tray rested about a foot above my wife's head. The woman turned and walked away. My wife, undaunted, reached up high to lift off the top tray. As I rounded into the far end of that aisle, I could see my wife trying to get her hands beneath that tray as she lifted it away. I had a perfect view of what happened next.

The plastic tray, not made to support the weight of this much fruit, buckled in the middle between my wife's hands held above her. This created a funnel for the fruit to follow the laws of gravity. Mounds of melon, pineapple and grapes came cascading in a great rush down the tray, bouncing off my wife and onto the floor. More significantly, large amounts of accumulated watermelon juice poured like a torrential waterfall down the front of the wedding dress, landing on the wedding sandals, before flowing off toward Lake Erie.

The store manager was full of apologies, as if this were his fault when it wasn't at all. I wonder if God ever felt like that manager, trying to rectify the problems of a world full of imperfect people. And does that make the deli worker to be God's employee, moving with the slow and detached unconcern of someone with a serious hangover, now bristling to the manager, "They ordered fruit of the Spirit, didn't they? Did they think they could keep such fruit under control: *love* boxed up, *joy* contained, *patience* served on a toothpick, *kindness* and *generosity* measured out piece by piece[6]? Haven't they been praying for blessings to be poured out upon this wedding? Don't they know that these fruits of the Spirit come not in manageable portions but by the bursting bucketful? And that melon looked good on her."

My wife took it all in good humor, predictably, although she was a bit concerned that at an outdoor wedding she might draw flies. Some careful sponging of the dress did wonders with the watermelon juice. All in all, it was a day of being showered with blessing from above – as long as you did not mind watermelon sandals making your toes stick together.

---

[6] Galatians 5:22-23

HUMILITY

HUMILITY IS SUCH A TIGHT FIT. Doesn't it always seem to be a size too small? About 15 years into being a pastor, I visited a hospitalized young man near his college. Having seated myself at the bedside, we were in the midst of a leisurely conversation about school, health, basketball and such matters of heaven and earth. Into the room strode an older gentleman who greeted us all heartily and proceeded, having gained the floor, to occupy the podium. My first thought: this is medical personnel; let him conduct his business.

Soon I saw my error, for he was now discoursing on religion in general and his own ministry in particular, obviously a preacher. In the suddenness of all this, no introductions had been given, so I brilliantly (and wrongly) deduced this to be the pastor of a family member or a friend of the patient. Later I learned the family had no idea who he was. Who this man guessed me to be is uncertain, except that after some earnest remarks on the blessedness of God, the value of faith, and the intransigence of today's sinners, he turned to me and abruptly asked, *"Are you walking with Jesus?"*

"I am trying to," I replied uneasily, somewhat taken aback. Why is he asking me that? I am not the patient here. I am a pastor, clergy, for crying out loud. But he was now holding forth on the nature of his church, the challenge of his radio ministry, the joys of deer hunting, and the sorry spiritual state of so many. (Was he looking at me?) With that, he undertook a full and flowing prayer, touching on most any concern you would ever want to pray about including our patient's health and the spiritual awakening of any lost souls far or near, perhaps even sitting in this room.

Turning his farewell gaze upon me, he announced kindly, "I like you somehow. *Someday the Lord is going to lay a hand on you*, I believe." Then he was gone.

This was, of course, great entertainment to my patient, and if he did not benefit, it was no fault of the Clergy Guild.

My pastor's clothes, however, have seemed a bit snug ever since.

PEDIGREE

SOME YEARS AGO MY BROTHER AND I were separately headed on a Sunday afternoon toward the same destination. Our intergenerational mission trip and his youth mission group were to rendezvous at a West Virginia mission site. As we journeyed, we kept in communication with early era cell phones which in the hill country sort of worked.

Unfortunately, my brother's group had mechanical trouble with their rented van which stranded them. Phone calls back to the rental company were not proving to be helpful. At one point, my brother made yet another call to them with mounting frustration. Except that he dialed my number by mistake. Despite the poor cell phone reception, I knew my brother's voice, but he thought he had the manager of the rental company. As he described once again his situation, I was not forthcoming with apologies or solutions. When he continued to press me (thinking I was the rental guy) to resolve their dilemma of a broken-down van, I responded, "What can I do about it?" Or maybe it was "Why are you telling this to me?"

All observers to the conversation agree at this point my brother turned seven shades of apoplectic. Just as he was about to abandon negotiation and cut loose with adjectives and metaphors hitherto reserved for stubborn barnyard animals, a light dawned: "Randy?" That is to say, just when he was about to read to me my pedigree, we discovered that we had the same one.

It was a sober reminder. Christians know (though we may be reluctant to recall) that in the irritating encounter – with the maddening brother, the obnoxious telemarketer, the woman who crosses our path smelling of poverty, the president leading us into an ill-considered war, the other driver met today on the road – we share the same pedigree:

God's children all. *Sinners* all. *Forgiven* all. *God-beloved* all.

PARKING BRAKE

I ALWAYS USE THE PARKING BRAKE. Almost always. I just don't trust the combination of hillside and standard transmission. So to keep my car from departing without me at our hilltop parsonage, I religiously kick down that parking brake.

Why is it the one time you leave the windows open is when it rains? It was late winter; a light skiff of snow had frozen to the ground. I drove up the driveway, intent on a short stop at home. Since I was soon to leave again, I pulled up to the garage instead of parking inside. I almost always use the parking brake. Could I have possibly left the transmission in neutral or did it pop out of gear? You can perhaps visualize our hilltop parsonage with its spectacular view where the ground falls away on all sides, and the only thing flat about the property is the parking space behind the garage, which is an insult to the word "flat". Now the parking area was frozen hard and smooth, and as I stood there opening the basement door my ears froze to the crunching sound of slowly rolling tires.

I ran to catch up, but it was gathering momentum, that car rolling backwards. As it hit the serious slope, it mysteriously changed direction, thereby mercifully passing between a parked car and the goat shed. But now the only thing between our best car and the woods far below was the long, steep field. My wife, happening to glance out the kitchen window, saw our car pass before her eyes, and out of sight. I ran after it as if this were a disobedient puppy that might be made to heel. But there was nothing to be done.

"Trust in the Lord," proposes the psalmist over and over. That makes more and more sense to me, for life keeps getting away from me. I am not just referring to the realizations of having turned 40, but to

those things that keep rolling away and down the back forty. I make all these plans and goals but mostly life careens ahead, often flattening those well-laid notions. I trot along behind, telling myself that everything is under control and it will be alright. This is a half-truth. Very little in my life is under control for long, yet it will be surely alright because of God. *"I trust in thee, O Lord, I say, 'Thou art my God.' My times are in thy hand; deliver me..."*[7] That is what God does: make things alright, in God's own time and way.

We call it redemption. The worst does not always happen. There is a saving grace at work, even when life seems to have totally gotten away from us. I am still driving that car today. Can't quite explain it – part-way down the hill it repented. I mean it literally turned around, bumped into the hillside, appeared dangerously headed for the woods again, only to keep turning until it came to a stop sideways. I drove it away... told my wife everything was under control.

Friends, trust in the Lord. You cannot go through all of life with your parking brake on.

---

[7] Psalm 31

TAKE A HIKE

"You don't preach; you talk." That was the comment to me many years ago by a parishioner. And he was one who <u>liked</u> me. *You don't preach* – I took it to mean that my sermons lacked emotion, excitement, fervor, whooping – just talk. Guilty, without doubt. But now I am wondering if he was onto something else.

Preaching is this odd task of preparing the way of the Lord. People hopefully do not come to hear what *I* have to say. Just one attempt to thumb through an old sermon proves the folly of this, unless you are out of sleeping pills. I suppose sermons can appeal by entertaining or patronizing, or because of the magnificent use of language by an orator. But I don't call that preaching, and neither did my critic friend. Was he trying to help me see that Christian preaching is where God somehow speaks in the moment to the mind and heart of the worshiper? My talking was not helping that to happen for him.

The preacher explores the text, pokes a stick into it to measure its depth, looks around to see where it will lead, and with all this invites the listener to taste and see that the Lord is good. Preparing to preach is preparing the way for the Lord to speak in and through and around the preacher's words. Hearing the sermon is preparing to be spoken to by a word of grace and power beyond anything the preacher can muster. Listen for the word of the Lord.

Absent the preacher, this is what the Bible is for us: the word of God. That is not merely a respectful title (like the *Honorable* Senator, the *word of God* Bible). It really is the word of God. Sure, it is full of stories, poetry, letters, prophetic proclamations, and all manner of human literature easy and hard to understand. But the Christian experience is that God speaks in and through all this. God's word can come to you while reading an obscure part of Deuteronomy just as God's word may speak through the most obtuse sermon on Sunday morning.

Some treat the Bible as a sort of reference book for moral or spiritual direction. For others it is an answer book to reinforce their religious convictions. I would like to recommend the Bible as a **great place to take a hike**.

Take a hike; the Bible invites you into its space. Take a passage and walk around in it for a while. Explore its width and depth and breadth. Hike through its swamps and up its heights for the view. Sit down in it and listen. Interact with its characters and what they have to say. Spend the day with them. Take a hike through a Bible story, passage, or even a verse.

Listen for the word of God to you.

FUNERAL PROCESSION

Few things are more predictable than a funeral service. Oh, the people there may surprise you at times. But the funeral director profession has brought a planned procedure and orderliness that allow us to not only anticipate what will happen next, but what time we will arrive from the cemetery for the church dinner.

Imagine then my consternation when, as the procession drove off for the cemetery with my car ahead of the hearse and just behind the police escort, the hood latch opened. Well, not on its own, I pulled the hood release by mistake. The funeral home employee who lined up the vehicles had set the parking brake about halfway. Trying to free it while I drove, I released the hood instead of the parking brake. Oops. Fortunately, the secondary latch held the hood, loose but down. However, I had visions of leading a funeral procession down the road with my car hood flying high, blocking all vision before me, headed to who-knows-where.

I wonder if I could have kept on driving, peeking through that crack between open hood and exposed engine. I wonder how long that procession would have followed me. And would they all have followed suit by popping open their hoods as we processed?

Considering my life and yours, I think how impossible it is to keep life in line, how often the hood has popped up or threatened to do so, how easy it is to end up in a ditch through no great fault of our own. I think of how we need help, each other's help, God's help. I think of the help God promises. I think of stories, Bible stories, your stories you tell me, of how God delivers on those promises.

The longer I am at this ministry business, even though I learn a great deal, the less I seem to know for certain. But I do know that car hoods can come open at the most doggone times.

And this: the Lord will make a way somehow.

FLYING SANDBOX LIDS

Life's a rum thing. I begin the week with the odd knowledge that last night's burst of wind picked up the sandbox lid behind the house and bashed it against the side of our car. That is right, the sandbox lid, hundreds of dollars damage, smacking that car in three or four places. My insurance agent took it calmly. He wanted to know if the sandbox lid had been involved in any previous claims. No, my sandbox lid has no violent record, although it has been known to warp and trip running children. "Comprehensive coverage," testified my agent, "that is our insurance savior here." Presumably, *comprehensive* includes flying sandbox lids.

It appeared to be a harmless piece of plywood, that culprit sandbox lid. Life has a way of lashing out in sudden and unexpected ways, mocking us in our face not unlike an exploding cigar. Had the perpetrator been a person (sideswiping my car in a parking lot, for example), I would not have been surprised. I know human beings regularly damage their own lives and those of others. But the sandbox lid?

I considered transforming that sandbox lid into firewood. I may, still. Or nailing that sandbox shut forever. What then of flying chickens, bushel baskets, or clothespins? Life has more imagination than I have nails.

There is it, my need for God exposed. Only God can provide the full comprehensive coverage I need on myself. For I need someone to help me make sense of life's surprise twists. I need a way to comprehend the meaning and purpose and calling for my life in a blustery world. I need a Guardian to protect me from harm's unpredictable way, and a Savior to keep me from being a reckless and dangerous object in others' way. I need what only the God of Jesus Christ has shown the ability to do: keep me from going crazy in a world of flying sandbox lids.

DRY SPELL

It is too hot to meander today, too hot and too dry. The Bible School theme this month was *water* in the Bible and the word of God found in those watery events. Very timely: we need rain. The Bible has lots of stories involving water; maybe some of that will slosh over into our gardens and fields.

Egypt experienced a shortage of water in Joseph's time causing seven lean years of crops.[8] At least I assume water was the culprit. Those lean years followed seven plentiful years with bumper crops. You may recall that Joseph saved the day for Egypt by using his position in Pharaoh's government to stockpile surplus food during the good years. When the seven years of famine came, Joseph had enough stored for the people of Egypt and more to spare.

In my youth, I once tried a rain dance on the lawn to bring much needed showers for our dry farmland. Joseph took a longer view. He stored up grain for a time when it would be needed. I guess that is why we have reservoirs of water for our towns and cities, and at school a supply of extra pencils in hand, well-sharpened, for the big test.

What do you have stored up for a lean time to come? What do you have stockpiled in your heart and soul for the challenging moment, the time of testing? Perhaps your life is flourishing right now, or at least going along well enough, a time of plenty. But when the lean time comes, as it so often does, what do you have to fall back on?

What grains of faith are stored in your barn? What harvest of hope kept long ready for the famine? What do you have to see you through the dry spell?

---

[8] Joseph, son of Jacob – see Genesis 41

REST

Apparently God is a slacker. At least, that is what I hear. God created the heavens and the earth in six days and then took a day off, rested. You would think that God would have more stamina than that. Starting a new job, God could only go six days without needing a breather? All God did was create night and day, sun and moon and stars, land and seas, animals and people. I know of people who work a lot more than six days in a row, farmers at planting season for example, and company executives, and carnival roadies, and mothers. I wonder how God would handle those jobs.

By contrast, *Time* magazine just ran a cover story on how Americans are not using their allotted vacation days. Of course not! We have work to do, projects to complete, and a reputation to keep up for total dedication to our work. After all, do you want people saying you are busy as a beaver or that you are well rested? Would you prefer your job evaluation to read "hard working" or "good at taking days off"? Days off simply allow the work to stack up for when you get back. It is remarkable God did not notice that. Moreover, steady, all-in work is how we get ahead of, well, whomever we want behind us. On the seventh day, God rested. Lack of ambition, it would appear.

Not satisfied with resting alone, God decided we should rest as well. God was so focused on this that it became Commandment #4 in the Top Ten. "Remember the Sabbath and keep it holy. For six days you shall labor and do all your work. But the seventh day is a Sabbath to the Lord your God; you shall not do any work…"[9] That command

---

[9] Exodus 20:8-10

includes not just you but any family or workers for whom you are responsible. Has the Lord noticed that the lawn needs to be mowed?

What is this all about, anyway? Has this day of rest anything to do with our lives these days, or is it one of those Bible anachronisms like leaving a burnt offering on the altar?

What if this commandment is really a gift, something we do for God so that God can do something for us? Christians along the way begin to realize that the purpose of our lives and of creation itself is to reflect God's glory and goodness, and while we are at it, *to enjoy God.* We are to honor our Creator by enjoying this life and world that God has given us. We cannot do that if we are worn in body and spirit. Rest, so that you can enjoy the Creator's gifts not just on the seventh day but every day!

A wise one once told me that as pastor the congregation needed me not to run around doing everything but to be rested and ready for when they *really needed* me. Where is the day or season of rest in your life for the Lord to refresh you for how you are really needed, and to renew your body and soul to enjoy the days you have been given?

MISSED IT

My niece recently graduated from Ohio State University. It was a nice, intimate ceremony of perhaps 15,000 people or more in the football stadium. A U.S. Senator was the commencement speaker, and as an aspiring presidential candidate there was some excitement about that, but we couldn't have made out what he was saying from where we were seated even if we had arrived on time to hear him. Nevertheless, graduations are festive occasions, and I enjoyed it.

After my niece received her diploma and marched out of the stadium, the family gathered around her at one of the exits for the traditional backslapping and photo shoot.

I excused myself to find a bathroom. When I returned only moments later (no line in the men's restroom), the family reported that the Senator had just walked by and personally congratulated my niece. I said, "You've got to be kidding." No, they were all abuzz. The senator was quietly departing, came right alongside them, caught my niece's eye, and offered congratulations. Everyone was there and saw it. Except me, of course. My big chance to be up close to power and celebrity, and I was in the restroom. I'm not sure which my family enjoyed more – the senator's attention, or my missing it.

It got me to thinking. What if Jesus had walked by, and I missed him? I don't mean at Ohio Stadium, although I reckon he has season tickets. And I don't mean a sky-is-falling Second Coming, but what if Jesus stopped by for a few moments to see how it is going with some of his disciples, and I missed him? It could happen. Jesus must care how we are carrying on his work in his name. What if he dropped by to give a word of encouragement and blessing, and I missed him! I was Otherwise Occupied.

Grace and I went on from that graduation to join the Intergenerational Mission Trip to West Virginia. We painted a house. Now that would have been a good time for Jesus to come by, with me holding a ladder for someone, or with a paintbrush in my hand. But of course we cannot pick the moment. We might not even notice him. Like me, you might have wandered off right when he came along.

Have you thought about Jesus checking in on you, stopping by at some unexpected time? What would he find you doing? Would he find you *about his business* of befriending the poor and the lowly, forgiving one another, praying for your enemies, making peace with your brother or sister, and honoring your Creator?[10] Or, would it be that you had just ducked out?

---

[10] Luke 2:49 King James Version

GENEROUS SERVINGS

"The servings are very generous" was the word on this New Orleans restaurant. Our Disaster Relief Team was there for the ongoing recovery from Hurricane Katrina, working on homes and a church. By mid-week, *very generous* portions sounded good.

The restaurant server did not disappoint. She began by pouring a generous portion of ice water down my back. The entire pitcher-full, to be precise, as it tipped over from her serving platter and onto me. It was a thrilling moment. Soon she was back with the entrée, generously tipping a heaping plate of shrimp and fries onto the lap of the fellow across the table from me. Abundant generosity!

In New Orleans, one could still find bemoaning about the disaster which befell that community. But more obvious was the generosity. There was a generous amount of hope, and a spirit of determination. People were generous with their gratitude, strangers stopping their car or interrupting their walk to say "thank you" for coming to help. Church hosts generously prepared dinner for our entire team.

Could this be a lesson and guide as we move from one national woe to the next – economy, natural disaster, human disasters of war and terror – and how these and other woes affect us personally? Perhaps the right attitude for such a time is *generosity*. Too often in the past, such times have brought forth blame, bigotry, and the scapegoating of others. What if we choose instead to be generous?

What if our witness is to bring to troubled times a generous compassion, generous understanding and regard for the plight of others, and a generous mercy about the burdens each other bears? This may be our time to shine as Christians, a time to demonstrate the grace of God at work.

Think of the possibilities. We might enjoy spilling a bracing pitcher of compassionate faith down the necks of those who need it most.

PRAYER

"Prayer does not work for me." I have heard others say that. I have to agree. *Prayer does not work for me either.* I often wish it did. I believe in prayer. I actually do it. I pray regularly, religiously, devotedly, sometimes fervently. Probably I do not pray often enough or in the right way. Nevertheless, I pray – in gratitude. More often, I pray for God's help. I pray for myself, for you, about all kinds of things.

But it does not work for me. No one, after my prayer, has jumped out of the hospital bed and said, "Thanks, I'll go home now." Not yet has anyone risen from my prayer shouting, "Hallelujah! I'm healed!" No one (that I recall) has responded to my prayer, "I am a changed person." Despite my prayers, the wrong people keep getting elected. And the Tribe still cannot win a World Series. Prayer does not work for me.

But *God works for me.* "If God is for us, who can stand against us?" exclaims the Apostle Paul, "Will not the God who gave his own Son for us give us everything else? Who (or what) can separate us from God's love?"[11] God's love wants good for us. God works for us, doing for us what we cannot do for ourselves. This is who God is. Even where things go wrong and terribly bad, God is at work for good on our behalf. In prayer, God does not need my permission, but desires my trust.

No wonder that prayer does not work for me! It is not a means to an end. *Prayer is about God.* It is about trusting God, putting ourselves in God's hands, entrusting others to God's care. Prayer is less about working on God to do our will and more about trusting God to work on us and for us. Prayer is about giving ourselves over to God.

---

[11] Romans 8

Paul wrote that we are to "pray without ceasing."[12] But when he was confronted with a great personal problem, he prayed three times about it, then said that was enough.[13]

He meant that he had placed it in the hands of God, and that was more than enough.

I admit it: Prayer does not work for me. But God does. That is enough.

---

[12] 1 Thessalonians 5:17

[13] 2 Corinthians 12:7

GRACE RULES

I leaned back, and that was against the rules. Sitting on the park wall in a city which I was visiting was clearly acceptable, even encouraged. The park had been placed there for people's enjoyment, a respite place from offices and hubbub. At noon, folks sprawled on the grass, rested on benches under shade trees, or sat in the sun on the short, capped wall that encircled a fountain. I joined others on that wall with our boxed lunches. All this was pleasant and quite law-abiding.

I stretched back, however, resting my head on that wall, one foot propped up. Immediately a uniformed park officer was at my side, announcing, "Sir, you are not allowed to lie down on the wall." She was polite enough about rousting me. But what the heck? There was no sign posting this prohibition ("Thou shalt not lie down on this wall"). The wall was not crowded whereby I would be taking space from others. The officer did not look like someone who went around inventing rules for her amusement. Do you ever get too old for someone to make you feel like the 1st grade teacher has caught you chewing gum?

She did not arrest me, or fine me, but I still felt like an offender. Probably this was an anti-"bum" rule, but unspecified (I guess she knew one when she saw one).

How are you supposed to follow rules that are unstated? I think about this with newcomers to church, especially first time visitors at worship. What are the rules here that everyone else knows except the newcomer? They invite me to sit anywhere... except for which places they did not think to mention? They will not turn me away for how I am dressed... but what is range of acceptability which all the rest assume? I am warmly welcomed, but when it comes time to pray will we be jumping up, kneeling down, or sitting quite still? If I pray out loud will it call down an usher? What are the unstated rules here?

That question is often asked of Christian faith, and not just by newcomers. Church veterans, young and old, find themselves asking about the rules of Christianity. What are the un-posted rules of proper faith, rules about staying in God's saving grace? What would be considered lying down on the job? What will get me thrown out of Grace Park? What rules do I need to know to remain acceptable to God?

Often the hardest thing to believe in Christian faith is that there are no such rules. God does not own a rule-enforcement uniform. God's love is free-flowing. God's grace is unrestricted. God's salvation has no fine print. We are accepted not because we maintain acceptability, but because God names us, claims us, and in Jesus Christ makes us belong to God forever.

BEARINGS

As I stood with the family in the hospital's Intensive Care Unit, time seemed to stand still. Indeed, it seemed to have stopped altogether by the look of the wall clock and calendar. The clock on the wall of the ICU room was stuck at 8:42. The day calendar on the other wall was two days old. That did not stop us from regularly glancing at both, trying to get our bearings.

I am guessing that is how God looks at things here, from a perspective beyond time. I doubt that time means so very much to God, at least "time" as represented by our clever clocks and calendars. That makes me contemplate again how very little we know about God. You would assume it were otherwise considering how chummy with God some people seem to be and how knowledgeable about God's thoughts and opinions.

I cannot see that we know all that much about God. It is as if we, all of us, were in a cardboard box together and were assuming that what we observe inside that box is the same as what God sees and knows from outside the box. Rather embarrassing.

Our faith story speaks of God sending the Son into the box to be with us. The Son tells us about God and shows us by his love for us what God is like. The Son gives us the best and most profound revelation of who God is for us.

We seek that God today through *worship*. Worship is how we continue to know God directly, as we pray, praise, and listen for the word. At least that is the idea. While on vacation, I went to worship with a congregation that was The Trying Really Hard Church. I was greeted by four different people from entrance to sanctuary; every effort was made for my comfort and hospitality, including cappuccino; music matched the mood; visuals served those who needed more than the spoken word; a relaxed atmosphere exuded Christian friendliness; the service was well-paced, and communion was meaningfully offered. Worship that day had everything except, for me, God.

Possibly it was just me. Probably. But I left that day hungry. I could not find God anywhere in that well-tailored worship. Maybe they did not allow enough space. Maybe God was not speaking that day. Maybe the worship leaders and I simply did not click. Maybe my heart was not right. It was probably me.

I do know, however, what is supposed to happen in worship: we and God find each other. Worship at its best is coming into the presence of God. We present ourselves before the Presence. The cardboard box cracks open just a bit for us, enough to get our bearings, to perceive and know God, not thoroughly, not fully, a mere glimpse perhaps.

Yet what is there on this earth that rivals that glimpse?

HATE

At church camp one week, as we beat the steamy afternoon heat with a quiet, indoor, craft project, one young adult camper looked up from his crafty effort and pronounced, "You know you've created God in your own image when it turns out he hates the same people you do." I don't know if this young man heard and remembered that statement, or if his different ability prompted the insight.

It is true of course, embarrassingly true, tragically true: *You have created God in your own image when it turns out that God hates the same people that you hate.* It is easier to make God (in our believing) to think like we think and value what we value, than to remake ourselves into the spitting image of what God desires us to be. It is seductive to believe God must detest what we detest and hate those whom we hate.

This is one assumption that is very inclusive. It includes and captivates those of many political stripes and religious persuasions. It feeds off our fears and prejudices and those things we just do not understand about other people. We fear what we do not understand. We tend to hate what we fear. We assume God must agree with us.

Therefore, we hate with God's blessing. Whether we act on that hate or keep it in our hearts, it is a relief to think that God looks on with approval. In the name of God, or at least with the inner assurance of God's agreement, terrible things are perpetrated against the hated with a sense of righteousness.

The God we know in Jesus Christ will have none of this idolatry. We were created in the image of God and were meant to honor that. To then create God in our own image is the ultimate perversion. Christ shows us the truth: God responds to the world's fears not by hating those who may even deserve it, but with love that gives itself and if necessary sacrifices itself. God's answer was the cross – God in Christ "reconciling the world to God."[14]

Imagine a world in which we loved the same people that God loves, and acted on that love.

---

[14] 2 Corinthians 5

GETTING GOD'S GOAT

What God must put up with from us! It seems there is something in us that just wants to get God's goat. This brings to mind my goat.

My goat is also a stubborn and stiff-necked creature. I built her a nice shed, at which she is methodically chewing away, always on the support boards, until she would bring down her own house upon her. I give her good pasture, but when allowed her freedom, she heads straight for the tender and forbidden apple trees. Long ago, I had to exile her from the Garden of Eaten. Why such a sinner?

She is ungrateful, this goat. Take her a bucket of water on a very hot day, like as not she will sniff it and then tip the bucket over. Cantankerous cuss.

She is wasteful. Give her pasture and she proceeds to tromp around in circles, killing the grass until she leaves ringlets of bare earth. She seems quite satisfied that this is progress.

She is greedy and covetous. Specifically, she desires the cat chows normally just beyond her reach. She continually eyes them. When led from her pen, passing near the cat's bowl, she waits for a momentary slack in the chain then lunges for those chows, bracing herself against man and chain while greedily gulping another creature's food. Thou shalt not covet thy neighbor's cat chows.

This goat of mine will not be led, even for her own good. Especially for her own good. Always she is pulling and tugging, sometimes to go a different way, more often just not wanting to be led. I run outside into pouring rain and approaching lightning to bring her inside; she braces those front feet so that I have to pull her to the shed, and we both get soaking wet. Not enough sense to get in from the storm.

Why do I put up with this? Maybe because she is so much like people I know, stubborn, ungrateful, and cantankerous. Maybe it is that her lunging for what belongs to her neighbor seems so familiar. Perhaps it is because she has so much in common with human nature that tugs in the opposite direction from where God tries to lead. Is it that she is so much like me?

Maybe it is just that when I look for Jesus, he is usually to be found not among the righteous ones who have determined their own salvation and judged their neighbors as well. No, there Jesus is among the goats who know their need for mercy.

COOKING WITH JESUS

The congregation's interest in the welfare of my family during my wife's surgery and recovery was very kind. The food that came our way was much appreciated. Still, there comes a time when one must make do. I donned the chef's hat.

I never realized macaroni and cheese was such a fine art. Grace sat in the director's chair to talk me through the casserole pitfalls. But it was up to me. The pasta stopped here. Now, I believe in cooking with flair; what one lacks in ability and experience can often be disguised with flair and flourish. If pouring from two inches into the measuring cup is good, pouring from two feet is better. No timid egg-cracking for me, got to show that egg who is boss. Of course there is no egg in macaroni and cheese; I knew that. Flair! That is the important thing. It also keeps the spectators interested.

Boiling macaroni is not as easy as it looks. You have two variables here, the *macaroni* and the *water* (three, with the heat). The purpose, as I now understand it, is to keep the macaroni swimming in the boiling water while simultaneously keeping the boiling water in the pan. My wife explained the latter detail a fraction too late.

Then there is the cheese sauce. An especially tricky maneuver in this process involves a gravy shaker. I carefully placed some powdered milk and water in that shaker. Not missing a beat, I jammed the lid on that shaker and proceeded to shake, rattle, and roll. Not a drop leaked out. On the other hand, I could not get the lid off. No lid however it too tight for a Real Man, and though that lid put up a good fight, it was in the end no match for me. That is when the contents slurped out. Flew out, you might say.

Still, the key word is *flair* and remembering this, I added what was left to the sauce and never looked back. All this was hard on my wife, who was already in stitches.

"God is at work in all things for good," the first Christians tell us.[15] That must include my cooking. Bad things can happen on the stove and elsewhere in our lives. Accident, error and evil get into the mix as unwelcome ingredients. The disobeying of instructions happens. But in all things God is at work for good. God is present and at work turning what we and the world have concocted, however nasty, into something good and right and restored. This is a great relief to me and an amazing gift, the flair of God's promise to make all things ultimately come out right for people of faith.

When I placed the surprisingly passable casserole on the table, the family solemnly gathered around to marvel: God works in mysterious ways, wonders to perform.

---

[15] Romans 8

PART THREE:

Church

UGLY TOWELS

Many years ago, our family received the gift of some particularly ugly towels. It is not that we are so fashionable in our tastes; they were just ugly. Our first instinct was to pitch them out the back door. But of course we do not throw away anything. We could always use them for rough jobs like dragging them around the beach or pool. And guess what? Now our family photo album is full of those doggone towels: kids with wading pool and towels in the backyard, family with towels at the ocean, campsite in the mountains with towels drying on a line.

The same goes for an old quilt. We have some beautiful, handmade quilts on display or in the closet at home. But this one old quilt was given to us long ago with the blessing, "This is just a plain old quilt, just use it." So we used it, in the van, on picnics, at the beach, for football games. While the fine quilts sit at home, this plain one gets seen with us all over town.

Of such is Christ's church. The church which is Christ's living body today is not something beautiful kept back for a special occasion. The church is a bunch of rather unsightly-looking towels that go anywhere doing the most common and unspectacular service. The church is a plain old quilt that gets used by God for whatever need is at hand. That is to say, the church is us. God takes us common towels and wipes up the hurts that are spilled all around. God uses the plain quilt of our life together to piece together reconciliation out of the scraps of brokenness.

Here is a hope: when God's family album is finally unfolded, we will keep showing up in the pictures! And here is a wonder: ugly towels and plain quilts become God's most beloved and forever cherished.

BACKSIDE

Life can be prickly. This was brought home to me once again by personal illustration when a colleague and I took a break from an evangelism conference. Picture us heading down the road to our destination when I decide to get off our path and go through the bushes. Actually, they are cactus. Cacti. Prickly.

There is one kind of cactus of which its parts easily break off and attach themselves to whatever happens to be passing by. In this case, it is my rear end.

I cannot see this cactus on my backside, but somehow I must know it is there because I instinctively sweep my hand back to brush it off. Bad move. Now my hand is full of cactus thorns whose fishhook-like briars are embedded under the skin.

I am painfully pulling out these barbed thorns that are taking the skin with them, one finger swelling up and assuming an unnatural color, and I am not at all clear how to get rid of that cactus still clinging to my backside. I call to my colleague that I am in need of some help here. He says sure, just let him get a camera.

This is why we need the church. Christians need each other. That evangelism conference was focused on how with the Gospel we can engage people who feel they are doing fine by themselves or who believe in God but see no need for the church.

I felt the need. That is, we need each other. Life can be prickly. No matter how self-reliant we are, no matter how centered on the pathway of faith, there are times when we get sidetracked, off the path, and tangled up.

We need each other as Christians in the church to keep each other on the right path, and to help each other get unstuck when we stray. We also need one another with a camera to help us see ourselves, our situation from another perspective, life (so to speak) from the backside.

MOTEL

I had never been thrown out of a motel before. Informed there was no vacancy for me, yes, told I couldn't afford it, sure, but I had never been told to go away; that I was not wanted here.

We were on our way home from vacation, returning from a renewing time at the beach, with no overnight reservations pre-arranged. Consulting a travel guide, we phoned ahead to where we expected to be, come evening, a modest motel with a bed. Bad cell phone connections in the hills through which we were driving complicated the reservation process, as did a dropped call. English was not the first language of the proprietor, which led to convoluted conversation when the call did go through. There was some amused frustration on our part; it should not be this hard. The proprietor insisted on knowing our arrival time, and then argued we could not arrive at that hour given our present location. We were not sure what he wanted from us since he already had our credit card number. All this came with crackling phone and language difficulty.

We found the place just fine and right on time. Tired from the long drive, we bumbled a bit, entering the lobby, back outside, inside again -- did this annoy him? As my wife began to fill out the registration form, it occurred to me that perhaps we should first look at the room. That is still done, isn't it? When we made that request, the proprietor reached out and grabbed the registration form from my wife, tore it up, and said, *"You can go."* Not understanding, we persisted, "You mean go see the room? We will need a key." No, "YOU CAN GO." As in, *go away!*

And so we did. Perplexed: did we insult him in some way? Abashed: we were apparently judged to be poor prospects as lodgers. A bit indignant: we had just been thrown out of a motel!

Churches are ever studying in these days how to be friendly to newcomers and welcoming to all. I have no idea how often, due to misunderstanding, unintentional insult, or unexamined attitude we have instead said, "You can go." How often have folks felt dismissed – *you can go* – newcomers made to understand they do not belong here, or old-timers found there is no longer room for them? Have you had it happen to you?

I do know Jesus said, *Come!* "Come, you who are weary and heavy laden, and I will give you rest." And, "Let the children come to me and do not hinder them…" And, "Come, follow me."

Jesus also promised he has prepared a room for us.

Happily, the church is not to decide who can stay and who can go. Jesus makes it easy. We are to offer everyone a room key.

TEETERING

"I'm back in the saddle again," I echo the western songsters of old as I head back to church after time away. Except that I am driving a car, not a horse, and the horse I am thinking about had no saddle.

We were on a retreat about "wilderness spirituality," and the retreat center had riding horses. On this day, however, the saddles were left untouched. We would practice handling the horses while riding bareback. No problem. Actually, I thought I would just watch, but what I saw was my wife sitting on the back of that horse negotiating the barrels just fine. So that did it. Now for people like me (tall, probably a natural wrangler), they recommended I stand beside the horse, grab its mane, and swing my leg over with a little jump while pulling myself up. It would come to that.

But first, I thought I would try mounting that horse from the tail end. You know, with a bit of a run and jump, put my hands on the horse's rear end and land fully astride ready for action. I have seen it done in dozens of movie westerns. Zorro could do it. In fact, some 25-year old had just accomplished it earlier that day. I could see no reason why I could not as well. And it would certainly impress my wife, setting her heart palpitating.

So that is what I did, sort of. I was counting on an adrenaline rush for the run and spring-up. It did not arrive on time. I also expected the jump to actually lift my feet off the ground. Still, when I landed, there I was on the horse. Rather, the horse's rump. *Teetering* might be the word for it. Halfway on the rump of that patient horse, I could not move up to its back. Nor was I falling off backward. I paused there, teetering. Other clergy watching gave meaningful nods of encouragement. I believe my wife exclaimed, "My hero," though it came out a little like "be careful you don't hurt yourself."

There for a few horse-wrangling moments I was balanced halfway on that horse's rump, see-sawing between glory and dust. Imagine if the horse decided he had enough of this.

Now I am back at home where plenty of folks are teetering. Mine was a playful moment, but there is nothing funny about their dilemmas. They come to the church seeking help, with stories of barely hanging on and sometimes falling. Their stories are of empty cupboards, lost jobs, shut-off electricity, and home evictions. Their adrenaline is fear.

They ask for help. What they need is Jesus.

The love of Jesus for us was a bare-backed love, a suffering, sacrificial, self-giving love – a love that puts things right again. In the church we do what we can in Jesus' name. When more is needed, then by the grace of God we will do that too, praying for Jesus' love to put those for whom he died back in the saddle.

DELEGATING

When I was young, my father sent me forth on a tractor pulling a lime spreader over a field. My job was to spread the lime onto the soil. That I did. What he had not counted on was the wheel of that lime spreader getting tangled up with that tree in the fencerow.

When you delegate responsibility, you must live with the results. It is the efficient way to get things done. But there will be mistakes, errors of judgment, and different ideas of how to go about the task. You may end up thinking, "I should have just done it myself."

A bit of a shock it is, then, to read that about the first thing Jesus did was to call followers and begin to delegate responsibility. What began with Peter and Andrew turned into the church, assigned to carry on spreading the word about God's love, teaching God's ways, and healing broken lives. Now I have been in and around the church all my life. What was Jesus thinking? To entrust this responsibility to his followers in the church, well, in the immortal words of Barney Fife of Mayberry, "That's nuts!" Why didn't he just do it all himself?

Look at what has happened. These followers cannot get along with each other. Some deny him; others betray him. Most try their best, but it is not all that good. They get the message cockeyed. They mix the Gospel with their version of common sense. They make Jesus sound like a spruced up image of themselves. They add conditions to forgiveness and are baffled by grace. They fall into disunity and divide Christ with their bickering. Within their reach, the poor go uncared for, the hungry unfed, and the lost unfound. The one who comes seeking Jesus is ignored. The Gospel spreader keeps running into the fencerow tree. What was Jesus thinking?

And yet, followers of Jesus have given the message of God's transforming love to millions. Millions more have had their hunger fed, their thirst assuaged, and found a new home in the compassion of Christ's church. Forgiveness breaks out after all, and the most unlikely reconciliation just happens. Despite the preaching, God's word comes through. Despite their reluctance, followers dare to pray for enemies. Congregations great and small keep praying, keep singing, keep telling the message, and keep listening for God. They take to their places of work a new integrity. They bring to their families a renewed commitment. And many, when their faith is challenged, do not flinch.

Of all the miracles of Jesus, from walking on water to the raising of Lazarus, his greatest miracle is the church.

CHURCH BURGLAR

Someone broke into the church the other night. That is what we have been looking for: more people in this church! I hope it was a young adult; we want them. It makes me wonder, if we made the church harder to get into, would more people want to come? Perhaps if everyone was locked out unless they tithed, for example, folks would be more motivated to find out what is in there?

Our burglar did not break or take anything, as far as I know, or do any harm except to force the locks on the office door and safe. Apparently, this burglar was only after money and expected to find it behind locked doors.

While we did not dust for fingerprints, we do have some clues about Mr. or Ms. Burglar. There is good reason to believe the intruder is not from our community, since half the town knows where we hang the office key. Further, this seeker of money is surely not well acquainted with church life or would know that the only thing kept in church office safes are musty old reports and records. Equally clear, our visitor has not had access to recent treasurer reports or would not have bothered.

Will our bumbling burglar return to the scene of the crime? I hope so. Would that we all be accomplices to a new breaking and entering! Suppose God has given us this burglar to be the focus of our attention as a church, this one, and all who are spiritually and socially locked out.

Our call is to *get this burglar back into the church.* For our midnight visitor was right in sensing something valuable, a treasure beyond price, to be found here. This seeker just did not know what it is, or where to find it.

HANDS ON

Our dog of recent legend was a hands-on dog. That is, if you were relaxing in a chair, elbows on the armrest and hands drooping over the side, he would scooch under that hand until it rested on his head. He wanted your hand on him, petting him. Not just for momentary pleasure or approval, he wanted it to stay that way. He wanted you to keep your hand on him, to be physically connected with you. He was a parsonage dog, after all. He expected the laying on of hands.

We use that term, *the laying on of hands*, in a variety of ways. We say, "I wish I could lay my hands on that book, but I just don't know where it is." That is not what I mean here. Someone murmurs in teeth-clinched anger, "Just wait 'til I lay my hands on him." That's not it either.

In the church, *the laying on of hands* means something else altogether. It is part of the Confirmation rite when young people profess their faith. Some look a bit dubious when beforehand I advise them that as they kneel I (and maybe others) will lay hands on them! When a man or woman is ordained to Christian ministry, other clergy come forward and together lay hands on the kneeling candidate.

We do this for Biblical reasons. When Samaritans accepted the gospel and were baptized, Peter and John went and laid their hands on them, and the Samaritans received the Holy Spirit.[16] Ananias, a church leader, was sent by God to lay his hands on enemy-of-the-church Saul so that Saul was filled with the Holy Spirit and transformed into Christ's servant with the new name Paul.[17] The church at Antioch laid hands on

---

[16] Acts 8:17

[17] Acts 9:17

Barnabas and Paul, commissioning them as missionaries bearing the gospel.[18] Paul counseled a young Christian, Timothy, to not neglect the gift that was in Timothy, given through the laying on of hands by the church elders.[19]

The *laying on of hands* gives us the Holy Spirit, and the Spirit gives us the faith, ability and blessing that we need for whatever God would have us to be and do. It is the presence and power of God with us. It is powerful. It is for us all. No wonder that when we kneel for the laying on of hands, we do so with some concern. This is life-changing business. When you rise, human hands pull away, but the hand of God is still upon you. Wherever you go from now on, that hand will remain upon you.

Like my dog who has your hand on his head, so the Lord's hand is now on yours. That hand connects you, empowers you, guides and blesses your life until some unknown day when you will finally say, "Into your hand I commit my spirit."

---

[18] Acts 13:2-3

[19] 1 Timothy 4:14

RAINED OUT

The sermon got rained out last Sunday. That was a new one for me. I have had sermons blown about by a mighty wind, sermons that got lost in their own fog, and sermons that froze up before I could thaw the audience. But I never had one rained out, until now.

An outdoor worship seemed like a good idea, even on an overcast day. The tent gave shelter to quite a few from either sun or rain. However, the overflow crowd had at least as many seated outside the tent as underneath. When the rain abruptly began about halfway through the sermon, the only considerate thing to do was stop the preaching and bring the service to a prompt conclusion. As it turned out, once we had abandoned the sermon and moved on, the rain stopped, and the service could finish without haste.

But the preaching was rained out. Since a sermon is always a dance between the spoken words of the preacher and the unspoken Word of God at work in the hearts of the listeners, I suppose it would have done no good for me to keep talking while the congregation was distracted by a downpour and scurrying for cover.

Still, maybe I should have kept going. Maybe the rain was baptismal water. Maybe it was God's way of helping out a sermon that needed more watering. I was preaching on Ephesians, talking about the Christian's dress code – how we are to outfit ourselves in Christ-like attitude and behavior toward others, and how we need a Christian's armor against the spiritual powers of evil – when the water started falling. Did I miss my cue? Was this heaven's way of telling us that God would clothe us in the Christian's dress code, and that we need not look within ourselves, but up to God, for the grace and strength of Christian living?

Maybe this sermon was just way too friendly, conveying a too genial and obliging God. Maybe the sudden rain was meant to make us take off our Sunday shoes (so they not get soaked and ruined) and find ourselves in the presence of the Holy One. Maybe it intended to bring out the umbrellas, reminding us that we are always to be prepared for something to happen when we come before the Lord. Maybe it came to humble us; true worship may begin on our terms, but ends on God's terms. Maybe the rain was an alert that when we come to God with dry and thirsting souls, don't be surprised to go home drenched. Maybe that rain's purpose was to squish all of us together under the tent, to have those on the inside make room for those on the outside, showing us how it is when we are all brought together as one in the Spirit, covered by the tent of God's mercy.

Should I have kept preaching when the rain began? Or was it that God, as usual, with or without my words, was providing the message for those with ears to hear?

I did notice that the rain stopped in time for the offering.

LEAKY PULPIT

During a recent rain, a solitary leak appeared on the sanctuary ceiling, dripping down right onto the pulpit. Speculation has abounded since as to the significance that this leak should be exactly over the place where the preacher stands. "God must be agreeing that the sermons are getting a bit dry." "It's a sign that this preacher is washed up." And so forth. Some have been praying for a heavy rain to come on Sunday.

There is a water mark on the ceiling above the pulpit. Whatever else it may signify, it is a reminder of why we come to worship: "My soul thirsts for you (God) like a parched land." (*Psalm 143:6*) Our souls thirst. The spiritual water we need comes from the word of God. That spot is this reminder: if my soul is parched, the rest of me will not flourish for long.

The wet-spot-above-the-pulpit is also a reminder about preaching. Psalm 1 speaks of rooting ourselves in the word of God, like trees planted by streams of water. The word which we need flows from above. The preacher is to rightly preach the word. That is the preacher's sacred task, to convey the word of God, not assert opinion, vent a peeve, or offer therapy. Whether or not the sermon is clever, entertaining, or moving, the preacher is to speak God's word through interpreting the Scripture.

The water mark on the ceiling also announces that it is the congregation's task to listen for the word. Did you enjoy the sermon, find it agreeable? That is fine, but not necessary. Was it stumblingly spoken or, worse, offensive to you? No matter. This is the essential thing: *was the truth told*? The congregation's responsibility in preaching is to listen for the word, through the ear and through the heart. What does it say to you? What do you do with it?

We fixed the leak, but the water mark remains above the pulpit, a reminder of both our soul's thirst and the Living Water we need.

Or will we paint over it?

SAID WHAT?

"Pastor said..." Being quoted always takes me aback just a bit. I am not particularly quotable, or articulate for that matter. Silence is one of my gifts. Some have been known to wonder why it can take me so long to answer a direct question (until I do speak, and then they see why). I have heard of a preacher who cannot wait to hear what will come out of his own mouth next. I can (wait). I know what's coming.

Still, "Pastor said..." I hear this uttered surprisingly often. Sometimes it is a kind voice trying to make me feel included in the conversation. Then again, someone may be using the pastor's words to bolster an argument. They may simply be reporting a conversation. Or, less often, recalling a sermon for another's benefit.

"Pastor said..." Not a few times I have been jolted by what I hear that I said. Did I say that? Or was it something like that? Surely I was trying to say something different altogether. But that is what they heard. Did I express myself so poorly to be heard that way? Or were my words so filtered through the listener's own thoughts, opinions, and experiences that this is the way what I said came through to them?

I reckon that is just the way it is with human beings. We listen and hear imperfectly. We get along as best we can, making allowances for misunderstanding.

I am curious, however, how God deals with this problem, people who hear but do not listen, who listen but do not hear. Who hear what they expect God to say, and what they want to hear. "God said..." Really?

"God said... charity begins at home." (Where did God say that?) "God said... do unto others before they do it to you." (Huh?) "God said... the world will end next Tuesday." (What happened to "no one knows the time or day" but God?) "God said… an eye for an eye." (But were you listening later when God said to turn the other cheek?)

How did "*as we forgive those who sin against us*" turn into "don't get mad; just get even"? How did "*blessed are the meek*" turn into the self-esteem movement? When did "*the last shall be first*" give permission for butting into the head of the line? Or, "*I detest your solemn assemblies*" become a rationale for sleeping in on Sundays?

God knows our listening for the word of the Lord does not always mean we are hearing what God is saying.

Can this be the church for you: coming together to sharpen one another's listening and correct each other's hearing that what "God said" might get through to us?

INVERTEBRATE FOSSIL

I don't know about other states in this country, but our state has an official Invertebrate Fossil. You know, there is a state bird, state tree... well, now we have a state invertebrate fossil. It is the *isotelus*, a small marine animal from the Ordovician period, about 400-500 million years old, unearthed in 1919 near Dayton, Ohio.

A **fossil** is some impression or trace of an animal or plant of ages past that has been preserved in the earth's crust. The dictionary also says a fossil may be a person whose views are outmoded, an old fogey. **Invertebrate** means having no backbone.

Reports have it that a number of politicians were considered for nomination for Invertebrate Fossil. But that is cheap humor. I figure a strong candidate must have been the *church*. Surely the church at times seems very much an invertebrate fossil, the traces and remains of something long since dead. And without backbone!

The church often appears to be fossilized. Much of the language and ritual is very old indeed. Church bureaucracy too frequently gives the impression of something that once had life. It can take the church forever, more or less, to get anything done. The preacher graduated Cro-Magnon. And what about invertebrate! By the time we keep everybody happy, the backbone is gone. Bold witness, daring deeds, and reckless faith are misplaced among the files of old bulletins.

What kept us from being elected official Invertebrate Fossil, our saving grace, is that there is more to the church than meets the eye. There is a deeper Spirit at work here. If the church does appear old and fossilized, it is with a Spirit that recalls old meanings and ancient promises which strangely stir the soul and warm the heart. If the church sometimes seems spineless, there is yet an abiding Spirit that causes us, despite ourselves, to stand upright. This Spirit becomes the backbone we lack, the vitality we need.

It is this Spirit which calls us into the church, making the church's possibilities for us outweigh the invertebrate fossil within us.

FRIENDS

For over three decades and most of its existence, I have been part of a remarkable church camp. Now called the *Hand in Hand* camp, the idea from the start was to offer a church camping opportunity to young people in their teens and twenties who had a developmental disability.

This was ground-breaking stuff, award winning back in those early days. The camp also invited teenagers without such disabilities to join the week as campers, giving them new understanding of individuals who were in this way different from them and making an interesting mix for the week together.

Many of our campers return year after year. One has come every year from the beginning, starting at the age of 17, now 55 years old. The camp is still planned for youth – and the young at heart who continue to come back. We have seen considerable social change through these years involving people with what are presently called developmental disabilities. When the camp was first organized, such folk were termed mentally retarded, then they became mentally handicapped, mentally disabled, people with disabilities, intellectually challenged, differently-abled, and an ever-evolving variety of classifications since. We just called each other by our Christian names.

The thing is that we got to know each other as people. We became friends. Maybe this is like no other circle of friends in our lives, but it is friendship no less. Year after year we have watched each other grow and change. We learned one another's eccentricities. We shared some adventures. We became friends. Others have often been complimentary of us as leaders for our efforts with this camp, as if we are making some sacrifice or extraordinary effort. They do not understand; this is a gathering of friends. It is the best week of the year.

Jesus said to his disciples that he was calling them "friends." I don't know what they thought of that. But I am thinking: wouldn't it be something if all the people with differences in this world would just get to know each other as friends. I don't mean they should or could deny their differences or the problems that go with them. But what if the racially different, those who are ethnically at odds, the rich one and the poor one, those with different sexuality, the religiously opposite, those who come from strikingly varying cultures, those with disabilities and those without, got to know each other not as groups or causes, but as friends?

I cannot say just what would happen, or how the world would change. But I think that Jesus would like it. I think Jesus would like it a lot.

CREATURE

"I know you," announced the child in the row ahead of me at the community event. "You do?" I parried. "Yeah," he continued confidently, "you're the **creature**."

It could be that the very young man was simply mispronouncing "preacher". But it just as well could be that looking at me brought to his mind the creature of the black lagoon. In that he would not be alone.

Some people considerably older than he seem to see a pastor as *the creature*, that not quite identifiable species in whose presence they are clearly uneasy. Confronted by chance with this clergy creature at a ball game, hospital, or supermarket, they cannot help blurting out half-hearted excuses for their long absence from worship or self-consciously offer some weak joke about their lack of faithfulness.

Others in the presence of *the creature* are reminded of some black lagoon church experience from their past which convinced them that the church is nothing more than a dismal swamp – lifeless, stagnant, even dangerous – to be avoided.

They have it all wrong. The pastor is neither truant officer tracking down those who play hooky, nor bookkeeper who keeps score of others' sins. As worship leader, the pastor is more like a conductor and the congregation the orchestra; if you have been absent for a week or year, take it up with the Audience, who is God.

As for your dismal swamp church, know that whatever your experience causing you to flee, that lagoon is not Christ's church. Christ's church is true to its name. It represents him, functioning as Christ's body in this world. It is filled with his Spirit. Such a church is brimming with life and vitality, teeming with joy, and pulsing with hope. Here you are fed and forgiven, find rest and faith's challenge, a place for all people from toddler to codger, from devout to doubter. It is where we meet the truth.

Come to think of it though, the child was right. I am the creature. As are we all: *creatures* who need to discover and acknowledge our Creator, and accept the costs and joys of serving the One who made us, redeemed us, and sustains us. Wherever this happens is church.

FAUCETS

A gleeful congregation could finally say outright what they had been sure of for some time, that I am all wet. The moment was a Sunday morning, at a church kitchen sink, where I was innocently drawing water when the faucet suddenly fell off, leaving a geyser of water spraying all over the room... and me.

After appointing a committee to study the problem, I finally decided to turn off the valve. By then I was noticeably soggy, as observers appropriately noted with clever comments. Their only improvement on the happy situation would have made this a Baptism Sunday.

Baptism is the grace of God washing over us. How interesting for the pastor to get the backwash! I was left wondering, as I dried off and mopped up, whether that spraying geyser of water does not after all represent the grace of God. Here is a spontaneous baptism of God's grace, spraying us with love, soaking us in mercy.

And what do we do? We put a faucet on it, a faucet with handles to turn it off and on, as if God's grace is ours to obtain when we wish and limit as we think best. Here is this marvelous and boundless gift that we assume to control by our own idea of justice, categories of sin, and measure of who deserves it. Even the church has been tempted to do this, to put a faucet on God's grace and dispense it on our own terms.

The lesson soaked into me: God is a free Spirit. The wind of God blows where it will. Waters of mercy, forgiveness, and compassion erupt from a deeper wisdom. The faucet falls off. Grace sprays us, God's grace washing us with unexpected blessing.

May your faucets fall off soon.

OWNER

The phone rang early Sunday morning at the church as I arrived to prepare for worship, arm-laden, rushing to awkwardly unlock the door and answer the call. "May I speak to the owner?" the voice inquired. Yes, telemarketer.

This caller knew the name of our church and that a church would likely be open on Sunday. I did not find out what she was selling (or buying?). The conversation was brief ("Owner? This is a church!"). Whom did she expect to be the *owner* here at the church?

Later, I reconsidered. Did she know it happened to be Pentecost, birthday of the church, the day that the Owner called the church into being through the giving of the Holy Spirit? Did she take for granted that she could reach the owner via us, the people who work and serve here on behalf of the Owner? I thought she was on the wrong page. But maybe she did want to talk with the church's *Owner*.

When we come to the church, we do expect to talk to the Owner, don't we? We are here for the One to whom our lives belong, and who owns the church. On a Sunday morning in the sanctuary we are looking to be in touch with the Owner. This should be a caution for us not to get lost in our rituals of worship and methods of welcome, nor become distracted by style of worship and preferences of music, and forget why folks deep down are here – to talk with the Owner.

When the caller asked for the owner, what would have happened if I had said, "You can have an appointment at 10:00 AM today. The *Owner* will meet with you then!"

CHANGE

"Everything changes," observed Heraclitus, ancient Greek philosopher. "On the contrary," argued Parmenides, another Greek, "nothing changes!"

"You cannot step into the same river twice," insisted Heraclitus. "Don't kid yourself," replied Parmenides, "you cannot even step into it *once*." Nothing changes.

So it goes. "Nothing stays the same," we note wisely. But then again, "the more things change, the more they stay the same." And, "some things never change." Didn't know you were a philosopher?

I hate change. Especially about things which I don't want changed. Then again, some days I am ready to chuck the whole thing out the window and start over.

The church shares those mixed emotions, resisting change because our traditions and customs signify the age-old reliability of Christian faith. Yet the church survives by reforming itself to keep up with the world's challenges. The Gospel itself stands on both legs: a steadfast God whose love is **unchanging**; a transforming Spirit who **makes all things new!**

When Jesus came along, the *Try Something New* crowd resented the respect which Jesus gave to the old ways. The *Over My Dead Body* bunch worried over his new ideas. But when Jesus announced he would honor the old ways by changing their lives inside out so they could turn the world upside down, they joined forces. They conspired that the only way God could try something new with them would be over Jesus' dead body.

As to that, not much has changed. In church congregations, the forces of tradition and the forces of change each play their hand. But the hand of God trumps them both, summoning and leading us where God wants us to go.

Are you following the leader?

CHURCH CAMP

The "Johnny Appleseed" grace is not what I remember from my youth at church camp.

That grace in song has certainly been a continuing theme in my adulthood as a church camp director for some three decades. But what stays with me from my youthful days is something else.

As a 12-year-old, I sat on a hillside during evening vespers singing, *"Every man 'neath his vine and fig tree, shall live in peace and unafraid. And into ploughshares turn their swords; nations shall learn war no more."* This "Vine and Fig Tree" song quoting the prophet Micah to a simple folk tune is largely lost, a casualty of musical tastes, inclusive language concerns, and cynicism. But it gave me an imagination of what could be true in this world because God wanted it to be: every person to live in peace and without fear. It introduced to me the notion that the Bible is not just about past stories and present moralities, but about a future that belongs to God. It suggested to me the faith foundation of living with hope.

At church camp, I discovered some things about the church. I met some young clergy and older adults and a raft of youth that came in great variety with quite different interests than I, but who shared a common dedication to the church. It occurred to me that *church* was a much bigger picture than the congregation I knew back home. I also found at church camp pastors and leaders who were playful and whose faith was full of laughter. I never recovered from that joy.

In the quiet of prayers around the Templed Hills campfire, the darkness at our backs, the deep stillness all around, I sensed the presence of God. The thought took root that God not only created, but is still present to us in creation. Does that mean (I began to frame the question) God cares about this world entrusted to us, that God is still creating, that God is still forming me? Could it mean that God has something for me to be and do?

Questions for the soul spit from a crackling campfire.

GOBSMACKED

Every once in a while I am *gobsmacked*. That is a British word which means "astonished, speechless in surprise". I am gobsmacked when I step back to consider the state of the church and the fruits of my labors.

No matter how healthy and blessed the congregation appears to be, I am always *gobsmacked* by how little that has to do with me. The review of our church's rather wonderful ministries and mission parades past, while my Big Ideas and Great Intentions can be seen still twiddling their thumbs in the corner. The blessings that grace our congregational life are just that – blessings from God by the grace of God. The faith and growth, devotion, witness and service found here are gifts from God empowered by the Holy Spirit among us. Yes, the Spirit may use our words or efforts (including my own) for God's own purposes, but looking back in review I notice how little the outcome is about me. I am gobsmacked and humbled by the truth.

At the same time, I am doubly gobsmacked by hope. Those who closely follow the successes and failures of the church find many reasons for concern. I need not detail them here: losses and lapses, things we meant to do but didn't, things that did not work out. Failures and fissures pour down like a summer thunderstorm. Humility can give way to discouragement. But hope gobsmacks me. Hope is buoyant, even when it should not be and has no reason to be. Hope that comes from God's goodness gobsmacks my dark mood.

Or should I say *Godsmacks*? Just when I am feeling the weight of my own importance while stocking up on responsibility and worry, I am Godsmacked with humility and hope.

Have you been *Godsmacked* lately?

LETTING GOD HAVE IT

Some people would really like to let God have it. I think that is a good idea.

Some do <u>not</u> want to let God have it. As in the old story (so old you may not have heard it) of the preacher who after Sunday worship would take the offering plate and vigorously toss its contents high in the air. The preacher explained, "It all goes to God. What comes back down is for me." Some do not want to let God have it.

Reasons why people do not come to church: they do not like to hear God say, "That is mine. That is my nickel, my dollar ... that is my wallet/purse you are carrying, my $50 bill tucked away for an emergency. That is my pew where you are sitting (it's bad enough when another human claims it) ... my carpet, my sanctuary. That's my car you are driving home... that's my house you live in, my dishwasher, my lawnmower, my big screen TV. That's my bank account with your name on it. Your spouse is mine, your children mine; you are mine." People do not like to hear this – God talking about creation in this way.

Reasons why people come to church: to hear God say, "That's mine." To your grief, "That is mine". Worry over a child, "That's mine". Your marriage strife... "Mine". The anxiety over a job, "That belongs to me". Your stress and pressures, "I'll take that". Financial woes, "Mine". Loneliness, "Leave that with me." Your fear, "That is mine." People like to hear God say, "I have redeemed you, I have called you by name – you are mine."[20]

They tell me it is *stewardship* time, which is certainly true since it is always stewardship time. They expect me to say something about

---

[20] Isaiah 43:1

money. You know, about giving money. How about this: What if we considered our giving money to be part of giving ourselves over to God – giving our money along with our worry and fears and grief and woes and strife – "giving" not as spiritual taxation but as the great relief of letting God claim what belongs to God?

Or, what I call **letting God have it.**

HYPOCRITES

"The church is full of hypocrites," asserts the long-standing objection to the church. Riddled with hypocrites – many seem to use this as a reason for staying away. It comes out of a certain view (incorrect, I think) of what makes a church, raising doubts in this way: "If Christianity is true, why are not all Christians obviously nicer and better than all non-Christians?"

With some help from C.S. Lewis [Mere Christianity], I would answer:

1. Christians test out to be neither 100%, nor 0%, Christian; rather, there are many who are slowly ceasing to be Christians but who still call themselves by that name, and there are many who are slowly becoming Christians though they do not yet consider themselves to be one. And many people in between. But all of us are complicated.

2. Unworthy people belong in church. From the first, Jesus has a way of attracting people whom others consider to be unworthy. Here is a different idea of church. Not a club for the spiritually arrived, the church is more a training ground, a place where 50% Christians and 20% Christians go for the spiritual food they know they need.

3. You say that church people do not seem to be any nicer than anybody else? Right! The invitation of Christ is not to become *nice* but *new*. You do not always find nice men and women here because there are all kinds of us seeking to become new people,

God-transformed people. Etiquette lessons would be easier. The hard task of 20% and 50% Christians is to allow God to make us into new creatures.

4. If there is any real difference about unworthy people it may be that they have a head start over the nice guys. For they may more quickly realize we are all unworthy, sinners who have come short of the glory of God, and that we are renewed as children of God only by God's love and mercy.

Unworthy sinners in church, you have discovered? Hmmm, perhaps this is just the place for you! That we may seek together the ways of Christ.

COMMUNION

Was it inevitable? Sooner or later, had to happen? The bread had been blessed, broken, and distributed… the congregation bidden to eat. What comes next: the cup, naturally. I have done this a hundred of times. Cup in hand, turn to the congregation and invite them to drink. Hey, where is everybody's cup? Oops. They are still stacked on the communion table, dozens of small, grape juice-filled cups. I forgot to pass them out. Oops.

This happened on World Communion Sunday, when Christians the world over try to drink together the elusive cup of unity.

I wish that I could show you the congregational photo of faces I saw in that moment. Some were bemused, grinning with the God who long ago must have developed a sense of humor to deal with the likes of us. Some seemed to be perplexed, with trusting hearts searching around, sure that cup must be here someplace. Others appeared to be embarrassed for the pastor, an emotion of kindness. But most faces were calm, showing an assurance that whether or not the pastor got it together all would be well.

That photo of faces was as much a statement of faith as any creed or communion prayer or anything I said inviting us to eat and drink. The *lessons of those faces*, I hope, help redeem my oversight:

1) This is why you are invited to "come and get it" at the communion table itself. The clergy may be ordained assistants, but they cannot be depended upon to deliver the blessings of salvation or even to put in hand the nourishment you need. Christ always delivers personally.

2) You cannot drink a saving grace you do not have, but Jesus took care of that. The cup of blessing is now and ever within your reach, clergy notwithstanding.

3) When Jesus tells you against life's thirsts to drink up, the cup is always full.

SOGGY BOTTOMS

The parking lot was full as we arrived just in time for worship. "Here is a wonder," I thought, cruising the area along with others looking for a vacant spot to park. Here in this mountain vacationland on a summer morning there seemed to be way too many people for this quaint, lodge pole pine chapel. It was tempting, of course, just to leave and get on with our day, "Well, we tried." But my curiosity had kicked in. I manufactured a parking place.

Approaching the church door, we found ourselves bunched with other by now latecomers who were told the church was full. It was, occupied chairs spilling out the entryway onto the decking. We were invited however to sit on the outdoor benches set in rows along one side of the sanctuary. The greeter informed us that usually the windows were opened so that outside worshipers could hear and follow the service. Today, though, they were closed because the people inside were cold. We might have trouble hearing what was going on inside, she added, handing us a bulletin.

Some of us stayed. We sat on those wet benches (nighttime shower), choosing our seats carefully to avoid bench puddles, endeavoring to join in the service through the closed windows. The woman was right; we could not hear much through those windows. I made notes on my bulletin: *Outsiders cannot hear the Gospel because those inside are too cold.* We tried to hear. This "fellowship of soggy bottoms" seated on wet benches tried to help each other listen… sitting very still, not moving. People trying to hear the Gospel read and preached. Of course, there was the cell phone vibration… the hymn book I knocked over… the soft foot-tapping of the young man behind me… and the low-flying airplane.

We persisted. When the shuffling inside suggested people standing up, we stood. It was not always clear why. I did pick up on the reading of the Nicene Creed, and the other soggy bottom outsiders joined in. We could hear the hymn tunes on the organ, but could not much tell which verse they were singing inside, which made it interesting. The scripture readings I recognized as the standard texts for the week, but we could not understand the words. The hardly audible sermon was on forgiveness as far as I could tell, and the preacher seemed to be in favor of it. I jotted down more notes: *fellowship of the soggy bottoms...*

Finally came time for the sacrament of communion. We were invited inside. Communion there meant walking forward to the chancel and kneeling to receive the elements. By our turn to make our way up the single aisle to the front, dozens of insiders were endeavoring to return to their seats by that same way – cowboys, mid-western families, foreigners jostling together. Spunk was needed to elbow ahead for a taste of God's love. Another note: *rough and tumble communion.*

Worship is our most frequent and common means of pointing to the Gospel of Jesus Christ. It is our weekly testimony that invites others into this faith. Even so, I am not sure we know what we are doing. Who can tame the Spirit of God in the church's worship, or predict how the Spirit will move? Sometimes all we can do is throw open the windows for people to hear, share with them the fellowship of soggy bottoms, and invite them to elbow their way to the Table of blessing.

SHOWING UP

Woody Allen said that ninety percent of life is just showing up. I am coming to think that is also true of being a Christian.

There was a time when most everyone we knew would be in church on Sunday. Or so it seemed. Not anymore. Now there are many other things to do, and places to be, and obligations to fulfill. Moreover, fear of divine repercussions for not showing up at worship is no longer much of a motivator. The result: though people today may be no less faithful to God than their forebears, they tend to be less often at worship.

Worship used to be an ordinary thing for us to do on a Sunday. Now it is becoming extraordinary.

This turns *just showing up* into a statement of faith. Visitors speak of being impressed to find at worship friends and acquaintances from other areas of life. Children cannot but note what their parents believe to be important by their dedication to the worship of God. Your showing up for worship, along with others, strengthens those who are struggling and in doubt, those who need the rest of us to proclaim the faith, sing it and trust it for them. Your presence at the church's worship may unsettle a friend to come and see what he or she has been missing. New families are more likely to come back and explore the love of God if your family is here to do it with them.

Christians are expected to show up when forgiveness is called for, when compassion is needed, and when grace is the only answer. We are also expected to worship God as made known in Christ.

Jesus told us to be his witnesses, to give witness to the Gospel. This freaks out many of us. Don't make it harder than it is. It may be as simple as this: when it comes time for Christians to make ourselves known, *just show up.*

SERVANT

I should have kept my camera ready. The photo that eluded me occurred at the church picnic. As I walked around the corner of the church at evening's end, there beside the large, almost empty, five gallon homemade ice cream freezer sat a solitary figure. He was hunched over in quiet thought, elbows on knees, soup bowl in one hand, spoon in the other. He was cleaning up.

Looking up, he grinned as if to say, "Well, somebody has to Put It Away." And he was.

It seemed altogether right and fit. Someone did have to put it away – rinse the tub, dispose of the salty ice, put everything back in its place including the remaining ice cream. He had already labored earlier in preparing this gift. He had organized tub, ice, and those who cranked the ice cream machine, I suspect doing much of the cranking himself.

There is a phrase describing the Christian life: *to lead is to serve.* Leadership in the footsteps of Christ is service. This service is often awfully common stuff, such as lugging salty brine for proper disposal. To be a Christian leader is to take on much small, bothersome, and unrecognized work that may eventually result in some body or soul being served in the name of Christ. To be a Christian leader is to open oneself to the inconvenience of serving a greater Good in often very humble ways. True Christian leaders are at a premium.

Then again, being a servant is not without its rewards, even when serving ice cream. Especially when serving ice cream! Who can predict in what common form or flavor God will grace our souls?

Thus, my unrecorded snapshot: lone servant, spoon in hand, bent to his sacred task, cleaning up.

GARAGE DOOR

I thought the garage door was open when I put the car into reverse. This was many decades ago, but for some reason that memory still emerges from the Deep Tomb of Goofs where it was supposed to be safely buried. This must have been the lowest speed auto accident on record. A teenager, taking the family car to school that day for after-school activities, hops into the car, starts it up, and promptly backs into, and part-way through, the garage door.

The feeling is like unto no other. A level of stupidity is experienced that just cannot be adequately explained unless you have been there. I was sure that garage door was open. What does one say to one's father? He took it like a man, no, like a dad. I cannot even remember what he said, which goes to show how much mercy was involved.

Consider: because God is often spoken of as our Heavenly Parent, we may acquire our sense of who God is from our parents. For some this is a bane, a great obstacle to faith. But with other parents it becomes a blessing. That day I learned something about the mercy of God.

Even so, it is a difficult burden with which to live. I have considered forming a chapter of Garage Door Backers Anonymous, as I am sure there are others who secretly share my blundering ways. But then we have the *church* instead. I mean what is the church but a group of knuckleheads who cannot back their way out of a garage without busting down the door (said Jesus, "I am the door"), yet who have received mercy.

What is the church but a bunch of spiritual garage door backers who gather to thank God for not yelling at us, who encourage each other against our failures, and who dedicate ourselves to driving down those roads to which God calls us – celebrating that the Risen Christ now promises to open the door for us.

PART FOUR:

Seasons

ADVENT

ADVENT PIG

I have a pig in my laundry chute. No small pig, mind you. This ceramic intruder stands over two feet tall with a scarf around its neck and an old sock draped over its nose. A porker there is at the bottom of the laundry chute with unusual articles of clothing plopped on its head and hanging from its ears.

I don't know how it got there, although it does exactly resemble a pig I once left staring at the TV in my brother's living room, all decked out as a football fan ready for the game. Before that, it bears much similarity to a pig I discovered standing in our backyard birdfeeder. Even earlier, there was the pig that found its way into the family Christmas grab bag. How did it get there, that pig in my laundry chute? It is too big to slide down the chute, and nobody here noticed it walking into the house.

Call it our Advent Pig. *Advent* is this time before Christmas, a time of waiting for the unexpected, watching for a strange visitation, and anticipating promises to be fulfilled in surprising ways. Advent deals in mystery and surprise. Advent is about a gift we did not know we wanted and never thought to ask for, but is just what we needed.

I bet you need an Advent Pig. No laundry chute, you say? Then how about finding one in the coat closet? Or seat belted in your rearview mirror? Or sitting in your pew at church? You definitely require an Advent Pig. Get ready for what you never expected to see in your lifetime. Watch for what God is about to do in places you never thought possible.

Advent puts us on the edge of mysterious intrusion and surprising arrival: a pig in a laundry chute; Santa sliding down the chimney; a God-sent baby in a stable.

SOAKED

There I was on an airplane, sitting in a puddle of Coca Cola. Airplane seats, as you may know, are designed by professional sardines. Seating consultants for the industry are Crabby Adults who are going to make sure that you finally "sit still." I am packed into the middle seat in the row, knees locked against the seat in front of me, staving off claustrophobia by reading and sipping the complementary drink.

As I am soaking up the novel, the beverage decides to do a little soaking of its own, somehow tipping over right toward me. Creatively, it did not simply plop onto my lap but landed on the edge of the upholstered seat and flowed down under my personal seat. Ever try to jump up quickly in an airplane? After you get the seat belt loose? I tried to avoid the sticky mess, but one can only stay airborne so long, even in an airplane.

I finished the trip sitting in a puddle of Coke. Not one of my more distinguished moments. Somehow, strange as it may seem, the feeling was not unfamiliar. I live and work with people who regularly find themselves up to their seats in sticky messes, embarrassing situations, and uncomfortable puddles of every kind. For some it is a relationship spill, for others a puddle of guilt or grief or indecision. For still others it is stress that has soaked into them and weighs them down.

The saving grace: we landed. We reached the destination. I got to stand up, move on. God does not protect us from every puddle we sit in, but God does promise a destination and a new day. God offers to help us to stand, persevere, and move on into that new day.

Advent finds the church awaiting something new, expecting a surprise that will somehow rescue us from our puddles and worse. May this Advent be such a saving grace for you!

And may its promise soak into that person who today is sitting in that airplane seat.

HOPE

This is the season for **hope.** Think not just of the desires of children, but the longing of all those who live in darkness. This is a time for hope even in the most hopeless of situations.

I am fascinated by the story of Rabbi Hugo Gryn. During his childhood, he and his family were imprisoned by the Nazis in Auschwitz concentration camp. They were Orthodox Jews, and despite the danger Hugo's father insisted that they observe the Sabbath and the Jewish festivals. A day came when in order to observe the Sabbath, his father took a piece of string and put it in a bit of butter, then lit it to make a *Shabbat* candle. Hugo furiously protested to his father, "That is all the butter we have!" His father replied, "Without food we can live for weeks. But we cannot live for a minute without hope."

Our hope is given birth at Christmas: Jesus, the Son of God whose birth into this world is light into our darkness. Jesus, who taught us how to live. Jesus, whose death made straight the highway home to God. Jesus, whose resurrection takes away our fear of death. Jesus, Savior of the world and Transformer of hopeless circumstances. Jesus – whose birth is hope.

Can we truly live for a minute without this hope?

CANDLES

Of all the things I enjoy about Christmas, heading the list are the Advent candles. Well before Christmas is fully on my radar, I am scrounging in the attic for the old candle holder cut from a slice of log by a parishioner in our first year of ministry. I search the stores for the proper candles which always need masking tape added to their base in order to fit that candle holder. In a place of prominence in our home, the Advent candles recall those glorious nights when children's voices circled 'round to read the Scripture and sing the carols… sing and sing and sing. The candles and their tipped flames point ahead with the promise of songs yet to be sung. Most of all, their light piercing the present darkness brings hope for today.

December is a time for activity – preparations for a holiday… making, buying, and wrapping gifts… family gatherings and office parties… celebrations and festivities religious and otherwise. *Advent* shares this part of the calendar, but offers a different sort of season. Advent is a time for waiting.

Watchful waiting: Advent is sitting early in the morning by the window and looking for signs of the dawn that you know must be coming but is taking its good old time. Advent is waiting for that name you cannot remember to pop into your head. It is waiting for the answer to the one-question exam to present itself. It is waiting in an Arkansas swamp for an ivory-billed woodpecker that most think no longer exists to nevertheless make an appearance. It is waiting not so patiently for the love of your life. Advent is waiting for God to act. It is a pregnant time.

Look into the flickering light of the Advent candles. You will see a worried parent searching the pantry for today's meal, a hundred individuals with applications in hand praying for a job around the next corner, a person visited by cancer looking heavenward for help... you will see in the candlelight a violated child running from the darkness, and war itself rearing its head above the fray looking for relief, while all Creation waits in its groaning for deliverance.

Look more closely yet – hope! Stare into the candles' light. Is that the sound of a trumpet, the word of an ancient prophet about to come true, the hand of God tearing open the heavens? What do you see? Is that God about to come down to save us? How about that star? Are those angels singing? Is that a baby?

TEXT MESSAGE

The young person from the doctor's office phoned requesting that I get a message to my wife: Arrive earlier for your appointment this afternoon. I said that I could text her that message, and would promptly do so, but I could not guarantee that my wife would see it in time.

The young voice on the phone seemed to be stunned. Why wouldn't a text be immediately seen and noted? I tried to explain that my wife was teaching at school, and that she might not even check her phone before heading for home.

Incredulous silence.

It turned out the message was received and the earlier appointment hour met. I consider this a triumph – I say *triumph* – for all who learned to keyboard on a typewriter. But today it is widely assumed that if a message is sent (by phone text) it will be immediately received and heard.

The **Advent** message has been more difficult to get through to people, heard and understood, no matter what device God used. Prophets were sent as personal messengers. Prophets such as Isaiah, Micah, and Zephaniah delivered their message and left the text for us in the Bible. "A young woman shall conceive and bear a son..." "For unto us a child is born, unto us a son is given..." "And his name shall be called 'Wonderful Counselor; Mighty God; the Prince of Peace'..." "Swords shall be beaten into plowshares, and spears into pruning hooks...." "And you, O Bethlehem..."

The message is of a different kind of Messiah than we expect or maybe even want, a different future than we now anticipate, and a different understanding of how God works and acts. And all this will depend on the birth of a baby.

HOW DO YOU KNOW

Sometimes my mouth and brain are not in sync. At times, my mouth gets ahead of my brain.

I had not been long in the new parish. This was my first funeral with the new church. Afterward, at the funeral luncheon, the two of us were standing together beverage in hand, chatting. He was a deacon in the church and the most influential member, as I soon came to understand. He was also the longtime church treasurer. Pastors do well to not get on the wrong side of treasurers in small churches.

A modest man, he made the offhand remark that he needed to shine his shoes. Now he was not tall, nor was he fat. But he did have a pot belly. So when standing there in profile he looked down and commented that he needed a shoeshine, I said, my 30-year-old mouth just said, "How would you know?" Looking down, how could he tell?

He was a Christian. He had a sense of humor. He did not shine his shoes on my backside. Instead, we soon built a friendship based not on impudent questions, but on respect and trust. Still, it was a close call.

Advent is at hand. People we hardly know, with names like Isaiah, Gabriel, and Matthew, will be standing alongside us, wassail in hand, telling us stories. These will be stories of hope and wonder: stories that expect God to do something great, stories of God at work in this world, stories of God acting at Bethlehem in an unbelievable way.

Bethlehem, birth – about this time your head may get ahead of your heart and ask, *"How do you know* this is true?" How can you tell if these stories of who Jesus is are to be believed?

The answer is not empirically derived; the scientific method does not work with this kind of truth. The answer is found in the stories themselves – in the stories of a birth, of God drawing near to us, of the hopes and fears of all the years meeting in Jesus.

How do you know it's true? Receive the Christmas story as a gift. Say "thank you". Try it on. Walk around in it. Wear it to work or school. You will soon know if it's a keeper. Is this gift *you*, like you were somehow made for each other? Do you feel right with it on? Could you wear it every day, for the rest of your life?

CHRISTMAS

PURPLE TIE

Someone gave me a purple necktie for Christmas. For Advent, actually: The note in the box said "you don't seem to have a tie that goes well with your purple stole during Advent." I received it too late to wear during Advent this year, although it will also do for Lent, *purple* for humility and repentance.

I do not know who gave this tie. Don't tell me, please; I like the mystery. The gift was unsigned, both nametag and note inside were computer generated. So there was no handwriting to recognize (or analyze). It was printed in red ink, which is a clue. The tie box was from Macy's, the tie itself a signature *Jerry Garcia* who was the lead musician for the "Grateful Dead" rock group and for whom the "Cherry Garcia" ice cream flavor was named. More clues, undoubtedly. The gift was left on my desk, therefore it was quite likely someone from this congregation, a person *who had access to the office*, and (here is where they slipped up) one who knew where to find my desk! Staff member? It does not fit their MO, although one has a known association with the color purple. A certain family does come to mind; they may crack under examination. Also, be alert for anyone humming "blessed be the **tie** that binds our hearts in Christian love." And where did I put my Sherlock hat?

This is certainly an appropriate gift for the season. Mystery! Advent anticipates God's act in the mystery that is Christmas. Isn't that what is behind all the candles and hush on Christmas Eve, the joy of Christmas Day, **mystery**? The mystery of God's coming that brings shepherds to a stable, kneeling, though they could not exactly tell you why. Mystery that makes the sky seem inexplicably alive with glorious song. Mystery that brings strange sojourners bearing gifts for an unprecedented birth they did not comprehend but were inspired to honor. Wonderful mystery.

The best thing about the Christmas story is that we can tell it, sing it, enact it, imagine it – but we cannot explain it. It's a mystery.

Afterwards in the stable, when the midnight visits of shepherds and magi were but a questionable memory, there on the straw were those mysterious gifts: gold, frankincense, myrrh... and a purple tie.

MYSTERY

When I first came to serve at Christ Church, it was Advent complete with cast. Angels, shepherds, innkeeper, and magi were all in place. Angels sang kind welcome, shepherds were holding the flock together, the innkeeper made clear my boundaries, and the magi...? One Wise Man told me to never say a negative word against football in this town. I am not making this up. A second Wise Man advised (or was it a shepherd pleading), whatever I do, don't change the Christmas Eve Candlelight Service!

Perhaps what I like best about Christmas is its familiarity and dependability. We know Christmas. Whatever the year has held and the new one might bring, Christmas is a fixed point. We can get our bearings with Christmas. That is the blessing of traditions, that they keep Christmas familiar and trustworthy. The tree goes here; dinner is of course at Grandma's. There will be nuts in my stocking. And if family traditions get disrupted by disease, death, or dispute, there is always Christmas Eve and its candlelight service – dependable, faithful, home.

Christmas is about what we know. The gift from Aunt Betty is not really a surprise no matter how outrageous or goofy. The stories of Mary, Joseph, and Jesus are as familiar as breathing. We know what to expect; the only question is whether Christmas this year will meet our expectations.

I want to offer you a Christmas present. It is an idea that won't stay wrapped: What if Christmas is not about what we know of God (good tidings delivered in familiar stories) but is at heart about what we don't know about God! What if Christmas is the marvelous gift of God's *mystery* and *glory* that we glimpse in Mary's story, thrilling our souls when angels sing, and making us run to Bethlehem with shepherds who do not understand what they are doing? What if Christmas is the blinding light that bursts forth when the swaddling cloths are pulled back to reveal the newborn?

I wish you such a Christmas of God's mystery and glory.

MIDNIGHT CLEAR

I think that my favorite Christmas carol is *It Came upon the Midnight Clear*. The tenor part is enjoyable to sing; the bass is within range for variation. And this carol hasn't yet been pounded into submission by the marketplace.

"Peace on earth, good will to… well, everybody," its glorious song announces. Who doesn't long for that? No empty hope, this comes from God, "heaven's all gracious King," and so we stop to listen, "the world in solemn stillness lay," to hear what angels sing. Do you hear it? Their music "floats o'er all the weary world," and that is a good thing. The world needs it.

Then it gets personal. You "beneath life's crushing load…" The message is for you, "O rest beside the weary road and hear the angels sing!" Pause and rest to hear the message: "Lo, the days are hastening on… when peace shall over all the earth its ancient splendors fling and the whole world send back the song which now the angels sing."

It just sounds like Christmas. Not a dreamy white Christmas, this sounds like the world you and I live in, with plenty of toil and weariness and crushing loads. And yet angels come and sing, bending low they sing of God's peace, peace on earth, peace for you. The words here do not name how that peace takes form: a baby, born in Bethlehem, a lowly birth. But we know how the glorious song of Christmas goes.

May it sing for you this year. May it sing to your heart.

MARY'S LAP

At the conclusion of our *Living Nativity* presentation during the downtown festivities, after the last robed shepherd walked away from the stable and into the warmth of the church basement, after the stage lights went down, after the manger and stage props were put away, and after the crowds who passed by on the sidewalk had gone, there were still signs of what had been. Sheep droppings could be seen in the yard, and there were cocoa stains on the pavement – signs of the Evangel.

We think of the signs of Christmas as being a startling star, angels singing in the heavens, and an unusual scent of frankincense in the air. But this year we could only manage one sheep for special effects. As for signs of the holy birth, careful observers could find sheep droppings and cocoa stains. Do not overlook their significance. While our *nativity* was staged, the sheep droppings were real, a sign of the Savior born into the nitty-gritty of our world. And the cocoa stains were the hard-won badge of our hospitality, as we invited young and old into the story of Christ's birth and the world of Christian hope.

My favorite moment was a young boy running up to the manger scene and climbing onto Mary's lap. He wanted to get a closer look at the baby Jesus, to be able to peer down into the manger. Mary's lap offered the vantage point he needed.

Isn't that what we would all like: to see as never before the Son of God in the manger? If we can no longer crawl onto Mary's lap, we can still kneel before the manger.

CONSTRUCTION ZONE

Our *Living Nativity* was set against the construction zone. I think I liked it better that way. The construction project at the front of our church building provided the backdrop for this year's representation of the nativity of Christ. The wooden representation of a stable sat directly in front of the chain link construction fence, which enclosed a backhoe, forklift, and a large hole. Dumpsters blocked the view from one side. When our Mary and Joseph took their places in the stable, they seemed small and out of place against the great equipment around them. When our shepherds came to see for themselves, they had to find their way past the dumpsters. And when our magi made their journey, it meant negotiating through stacks of lumber and concrete blocks.

Hundreds of pedestrians came by that night to stop and look: nativity amid a construction project. Actually, at that point it was more a destruction project, still tearing away the old in preparation for building the new. So they saw a portrayal of Jesus born into a world coming apart. There was the promise of something new and better to come. But what they observed was Jesus born into a world still under construction, in a stable right beside a dumpster.

It wasn't pretty. Nor suitable for a greeting card, most nativity pictures lack chain fence and backhoe. You had to walk through the mud to pet the lamb and to get to Jesus. Yet people did. They ignored the mud; they stood and stared at this unlikely birth in a stable at a construction site. It wasn't pretty; it was beautiful. It was a scene of *living nativity*, a witness of what it means that God is with us.

God is with you in whatever way your life is under construction.

BETHLEHEM GOAT

For this year's street-side *Living Nativity* tableau, we had a goat. Yes, goat. We don't exactly know what animals may have been present at the birth of Jesus. Sheep are traditional, given Luke's telling of shepherds who were watching their flocks that night. Donkey and camels can each make a claim as to why they could have been there. Goats? I recall no goats in manger-scenes-I-have-seen. Do you? No goats standing beside the shepherds, certainly no goats with the magi. But we had one: Mary, Joseph, shepherds, magi, baby Jesus, and goat.

This goat was very popular with young and old alike. On its bed of straw, it fit into the tableau just fine. Tame, and yet with goatish spunk, it drew people from the sidewalk to see it up close, pet it, talk to it. There was usually a huddle of people around the goat as if they also belonged in the tableau. All sorts of people from every walk of life were drawn to this goat until it seemed as though they were drawn right into the manger scene itself.

Suddenly we had a Live Nativity that was full of life. Not just portraying with strange costumes and representational characters a night long ago, this tableau had come alive. Townspeople were poking their heads into the stable, interacting with the cast: "Are you warm enough in that bathrobe?" "Hey, what are *you* doing here dressed as a Wise Man?" "Hungry, want a cookie?" "Where's the baby?" "Could I get a turn as a shepherd?"

It seemed like Jesus could have been born right there in our town along Main Street. The town was full of people and hubbub that night. Some were keeping watch over a flock of reindeer just down the street. Kids wearing balloon reindeer antlers came running to see the nativity for themselves. Others came bearing precious gifts, bags of popcorn.

Pictures were taken of the manger scene so that Matthew and Luke would not be the only witnesses. And right in the middle of it all was the goat.

It has been said, after all, that Jesus was born to be the scapegoat of the world. He came to take upon himself the sin of the world, including the blame and frustration and anger, so that we need not put that on each other. The scapegoat: *he was despised and rejected, a man of suffering who has borne our grief; he was wounded for our transgressions, bruised for our iniquities, upon him was the chastisement that made us whole.*[21]

A goat just belongs in the manger scene, doesn't it?

---

[21] Isaiah 53

CHRISTMAS PEACE

The stack of unwritten Christmas cards looms over the desk, taunting you. The tree you cut will not stand up straight once inside the house. Your dog is tangled up in the outdoor colored lights, now dragging them around the yard. The department store Santa looks as though he is ready to throttle that kid who keeps pulling at Santa's beard. The director of the Christmas pageant is on the phone, in tears. And your wife just walked in the door, having purchased for herself, on sale, the one good gift idea you had for her. In world news, another bomb exploded.

I know it is supposed to be the season of *peace*, a silent and holy time when peace comes to the foreground and strife recedes at least for the moment into the background. We glimpse how life could be, should be, will be, if we can believe the divine promises. So why are so many so stressed out so much of the time? Why does conflict seem to increase among us in this season? Why does one hear so many voices saying, "I sure am not looking forward to Christmas this year?" Why is this not necessarily *the most wonderful time of the year*?

I think there is just too much pressure. There is the pressure to come up with all those presents for all those people, gifts that are appropriate and "just what they wanted." There is pressure to do the family thing in the right way, maintain the traditions, add some joy, keep everybody happy and getting along with each other, and hope that nobody gets sick. There are the practical pressures of food and travel and houseguests with which to contend. There are the social pressures of school events, church happenings, parties with friends, and family get-togethers. But most of all, there is the pressure to tackle all this with **peace in our hearts** and, dang nabbit, **with each other**!

No one can thrive under this pressure, because peace is not something we can will to be. It is first of all a gift. The gift comes to you from God. The Bible talks about peace as *"Shalom,"* which is not simply the absence of conflict, but means the well-being of individual and community, with health and wholeness and joy and reconciliation all rolled up into one. *Shalom* is peace with justice and mercy. *Shalom* is peace on earth and peace of mind. The Christmas News is that *shalom* is Jesus Christ. He is our peace. The promise of *shalom* comes to us in the birth of Christ. He is our hope.

Instead of trying with holiday effort to squeeze peace into impossible Christmas boxes, what if we watched for Christ's peace in whatever way it might be delivered to us, down whatever chimney God is sending it into the world. Then look for how to offer that *shalom* – mercy, wholeness, well-being – to someone else.

Let God handle the pressure; you unwrap the joy.

HUMBUGS

Humbugs and hallelujahs...

Old Scrooge thinks Christmas is a humbug because, as near as he can figure, the world is a humbug. I suspect he is not alone. You may have had plenty of humbugs come your way lately. But a humbug-ish world does not mean that our Christmas pilgrimage of faith is futile.

You remember that Scrooge was to wait and watch for the ghosts of Christmas past, present and future to visit him. So the promise of Christmas invites us to anticipate and watch for how God will visit us in Christ to rescue us from past and present with the gift of a different future!

The mystery of Christmas has humbugs on the verge of unrehearsed hallelujahs. Get ready for some rejoicing, knowing that our Savior has a humble and even humorous sense of timing. When we are penning up the sheep for the night, angels appear! When we are putting supper on the table, strangely dressed magi on camels knock at the door to ask directions. When we are busily at work with holiday extravaganzas, a child is born in the back of the shed! When we can only see humbugs, a star appears overhead.

May Christmas bring unexpected hallelujahs to your life and home, and may your humbugs find themselves under the light of the star.

EPIPHANY

LEFT BEHIND

They did not know, of course, what the future would be. Mary and Joseph simply headed for Bethlehem. They had little choice in the matter. The Emperor had ordered it. What surprising joys and unexpected trials would find them were yet to be seen. The one surety was that Jesus would be with them, still secure in Mary's womb.

When Mary and Joseph found their way to the stable onstage, the manger awaited them. A somewhat distracted angel hovered nearby. Imaginary cattle were lowing, as was the audience in expectation. Mary and Joseph slowly took their places; they had no choice, the director had spoken. But where was the baby Jesus? Oops. The baby was still in the dressing room down the hallway, left alone on the table while everyone continued to play their parts. A mad dash by Joseph soon rectified the situation as he handed the baby over to Mary, much to the relief of the director and the delight of the audience.

It would not be the last time. Twelve years later, Jesus' parents would leave him behind at the temple during a visit to Jerusalem, only to later realize their mistake and make a mad dash back to find him. He was, of course, at the temple already about his Father's business.

Nor was that the final such time. Jesus' disciples left him behind when they tried to get out ahead of him and tell him his business. They left him behind when they jumped to the wrong conclusions about his power. They left him behind when they denied him, betrayed him, and abandoned him, fleeing into the night at his arrest. When Jesus was killed and the disciples thought it was all over, they left him behind.

We do not know what the future will bring. We take our places onstage and continue to play our parts: parent, student, employee, spouse, friend, and sojourner. We do what we are supposed to do. We do what we are called to do. But will we do it with Jesus? If he came to be with us, to be God's grace and blessing for us, will we let him? Will we take him along with us into the adventure ahead? Better: will we go along with him into the future?

Or will we look around and realize we have gone ahead and left him behind in the dressing room?

EVERYTHING

No matter how efficient we are at boxing up Christmas, there seems to be little time for rest and recuperation from our celebrating. Indeed, the real excitement is suddenly just ahead.

Jesus does not ease his way into ministry; it is full throttle. He comes out swinging. "Repent, for the kingdom of God is at hand" is the message with no warm-up-the-crowd anecdotes or getting-to-know-you period of time. As Mark's Gospel tells it, Jesus just bursts onto the scene and goes at it. He calls ordinary people to be disciples with an abrupt "follow me".

Do you suppose there were some who declined the invitation, ignoring the imperative? Did the first twelve people all say *yes*? How many did Jesus have to call until he filled the slate? I can imagine some responding, "Well, if you cannot find anyone else, then come back and ask me." Or, "I really can't this year; maybe next year I could leave everything behind and follow you."

It is that *leaving everything behind* part that gets in the way. Peter and Andrew immediately left their fishing nets and followed Jesus into a new vocation. James and John walked away from their boat and father to become Jesus' disciples. On the other hand, a rich young man later refused to first give away his wealth and then follow Jesus. He wanted it both ways, and I can't say that I blame him.

Evidently, to wholeheartedly follow Jesus involves leaving behind at least part of our present life. That goes even for those who have grown up in the church and in Christian homes. Following Jesus implies there are always about us things we need to put aside, give up, and leave behind – wealth, opinions, beliefs, loyalties. What are yours? *What is holding you back?*

Some folks worry whether they will be left behind when Jesus comes again. The more immediate question: what are you unwilling to leave behind in order to follow him now?

NEW YEAR

I have no idea what the new year will bring. Perhaps it will resemble past years as I thumb through the family journal.

"I like that Christmas tree," comments the two-year-old as the tree is being undecorated and taken down. Mom replies, "We will get another one at Christmas next year." "Can we?" exclaims the little one in sudden idea and hope that all this could be celebrated again. Whatever this New Year brings, at its end there will again be Christmas with its gift of God's love.

Now age three, the child kneels for a bedtime prayer, "Now I lay me down to sleep. I have a good chicken bone to keep." Whatever happens this year, there will be something for which we give God thanks.

Mom to a four-year-old, "You look like a million dollars!" Child to mom, "You look like nine dollars." Whatever happens this year, there will be plenty of occasions for humility.

A four-year-old stuffs homemade donuts into his mouth, musing "I wouldn't eat 10 donuts; that would make me sick. A person should have 5 donuts or something like that." Whatever happens this year, there will be an abundance of blessing in the grace of God.

Another four-year-old, at the County Fair, upon observing a cow drop a manure pie while being led into the show ring, declares, "That cow made a serious mistake." Whatever happens this year, there will be God cleaning up our mistakes with the forgiveness of grace.

The young one comes inside the house crying, "(Sibling) said I have no brain." Mom reassures child. Back outside goes the child, announcing, "Mom said I do too have a brain!" Whatever happens this year, there will be God our Creator reassuring us.

Mom to ten-year-old, "If you want us to go to a movie tonight, you will have to help clear the table for washing dishes – or do you expect us to wait on you hand and foot? Child: "Hmm, that's a tough choice." Whatever happens this year, there will be God to help us with tough decisions.

A five-year-old theologian, "New Year's Day is the day in olden times when Jesus was telling the people to be good... and they didn't like it." Whatever happens this year, there will be God to lead us, despite ourselves, in the right path.

So fear not! Whatever happens this year, at the end of it will be God.

STAND FAST

On the west coast of Scotland is the island of Iona, the place through which Christianity entered the British Isles some 1500 years ago. For many centuries, and now again, a religious community continued the presence of Celtic Christianity on Iona. From the old ruins, an ancient abbey is today being rebuilt. In the back of its completed sanctuary, off to one side, is a short staircase leading to a small meditation room just large enough for one person. The heavy wooden door to this room has carved into it the words, "*Stand Fast*".

Those seem to be just the right words for the New Year. *Stand fast* is the message to people who believe that the Savior has come, but who do not yet see the full effect. *Stand fast*, all who trust in God's promised new day even as much worldly evidence makes such trust seem foolhardy. *Stand fast*, you who are lonely and isolated, you who are hungry and hurting. Your redemption is at hand. *Stand fast* amid a warring and wearying world. *Stand fast*, for God has named and claimed you – you belong to God.

The irony on Iona is that the meditation room behind the wooden door is so small that once inside, I could not stand. The ceiling was not high enough for me, or most anyone, to stand there. In that spare, circular space was a kneeling cushion by a window that looked out over the island and water. The message seemed clear enough. The only way to *stand* is to kneel. To *stand fast* is to kneel before the presence of God. That is what the Wise Men did, bringing their gifts and themselves to the Christ. It is what the wise always do.

Stand fast in the hope that is found but not finished at the manger.

LENT

SOUL SCULPTURE

"*Lent* is coming," for many people their least favorite church season. Lent: the forty days before Easter, during which Christians traditionally prepare to honor Christ's suffering death and to receive the gift of Christ's resurrection. Prepare how? Repent, fast, deny yourself, don sackcloth and ashes!

No wonder Lent is unpopular. Besides, it seems irrelevant. Why *repent*? There is no use living in the past. *Fasting*? We have diets, thank you very much. *Sins*, we like to call them "problems"... we make "mistakes," and "bad choices," but we are basically OK, good enough. *Sackcloth and ashes*, we use Abercrombie and Fitch for spring fashion. *Self-denial*, say what? Lent seems so medieval.

The fact is my mind has already wandered to the bear sculpture on the nearby shelf. I sculpted that bear. Yep, back in college, in the tradition of liberal arts I who have no talent in art took a course in sculpture. I made a rabbit (proudly displayed by my sister, though come to think of it...), and a foot (presently exhibited in the Louvre or maybe garage attic by the louver). Was there also a nose? (Watch the flea markets for an unrecognized masterpiece.) Then there was the bear, which I created in the one hour final exam. I just followed the technique taught. As I remember, the key was to use very small balls of clay to build the base until it looked like the bear who was modeling.

Is this what Lent is supposed to be? God takes every little prayer, every acknowledgement of our shortcoming, every embarrassment to our pride, every admission that we have done what we ought not to have done and not done what we ought to have done, as well as every time we have thought of others instead of ourselves... and uses them like small balls of clay. God works with them and molds them until we are humble enough, honest enough about our sins, sorry enough, and self-denying enough, that God can sculpt into our souls the masterpiece of Easter.

ASHES AND DUST

The ashes are bad enough. Greasy smudge of burnt palm fronds mixed with oil applied to the forehead, they seem to attract a hand or sleeve, smearing and staining. Ashes on the forehead also invite questions, like, "Do you know you got into something?" We got into something alright. We got into the life of Christ, and it keeps messing with us.

The act of receiving ash on forehead is called *imposition* of ashes. It is an imposition. We are going along minding our own business, or that is what we tell ourselves, and these ashes shout out that we are God's business. Our lives are not our own. God imposes upon us great expectations, from loving our neighbor to taking up our own cross. The ashes are the test results.

They should be humbling; ashes have always indicated humility. Well, humility is fine for someone receiving an award, but what is this with wearing our failures and shortcomings on our foreheads? The point (of ashes) is to point us in a different direction for how we live, point us in the direction of God. But who likes someone telling us how to live our lives?

The ashes are bad enough.

Then there is the dust. Not actual particles, but the reminder: "Remember you are dust, and to dust you shall return." Real nice. Very cheery.

When folks shuffled their way across the carpet, coming toward me for the ashes, and I touched my ashen thumb to their forehead, a static shock surprised us both. Mortality is a shock. That is what the "dust to dust" is about. Remember your mortality.

I would rather not.

I know of course that I will die someday. But mostly I ignore the reality, categorize and file away the fact, in order to get on with practicalities of living. I have stuff to do, plan, enjoy – a new day to embrace, then a new day after that. And then another. There is no use living in anxiety or dread of death.

But there is something to being reminded of our mortality. We are never far from it. We are ever in the hands of God. That is good news. We are in the hands of the God who created us out of dust. We are in the hands of God who sustains us when our days want to crumble into dust. We are in the hands of God who will take the dust of our decay and resurrect a new body fit for the glory of God.

Remember you are dust, and to dust you shall return. Awesome.

SILENT PRAYER

Discussing the merits of *silent prayer* time during the church's Sunday worship, a young person gave this sage comment, "Too long at Silent Prayer might get into things you would rather not get into." Yep.

Thirty seconds of silent prayer together as a congregation can seem everlasting since: a) we are not used to sitting quietly alone without the companionship of TV, computer screen, or smartphone; b) we are certainly not accustomed to sitting quietly with others for very long; c) we are not much practiced in prayer that listens and then listens some more, allowing the Spirit to take us where it will. Such prayer is risky. It can open sealed off areas, throw light into well concealed nooks and crannies, and get us into things with God about our lives that we are not eager to get into.

Plumbing is like that, as far as I am concerned. You start out to replace a leaky washer and the next thing you know half of the bathroom is torn up because of what you keep discovering. The same is true with genealogical research: you might just get into things about your ancestors that you would rather not have known or brought to light.

Lent is this odd time which the church marks but the world prefers to ignore. The world likes our Christmas and Easter, both for the fun and the commercial advantages they bring. But *Lent* sits there untouched. Like an unidentified casserole (turkey, tofu?) at a banquet for vegetarians – they would just rather not get into it.

That also lets us have this Lenten season for what it is, unencumbered by the distractions of elves and stockings hung, of bunnies and colored eggs. Here is a time to be still before God. See Jesus for who he is, and not what we make of him. See ourselves as we are, including those things we would rather not get into. See God at work in those inner protected places with a love and mercy and healing that we could not have imagined.

Lent is our time for daring plenty of silent prayer.

FOLLOWING

Apparently, I look lost. Once in a while I do head off in the wrong direction, like the time I tried to drive home to Ohio late at night from a Pittsburgh ball game via Harrisburg, PA. Every time I tried to repent, turn around and rectify the situation, I found that I was once again headed for Harrisburg. Even when I am sure that I know where I am and where I am headed, people will stop and ask me with concern, "Can I help you find your way?" I must give off bewilderment.

There comes a time in the church year when we take stock of where we are headed. We get out our spiritual GPS and locate just where we are in the be-wilder-ness. Some do this with prayer and fasting. Others go about it with symbolic sacrifice, giving up television or chocolate. A few take on a new self-discipline: study of scripture or acts of compassion. Still others re-engage worship with new devotion. Each is asking: Where am I? How far have I drifted off course and not realized the full extent?

When Jesus left his wilderness, he set his face resolutely toward Jerusalem, and that is where he went. We are to follow him. That is to be the course on which our lives are set. Our working motto: *Follow the ways of Jesus, trust the promises of God.* Baptized and confirmed, now walk in the footsteps of Jesus. He is showing the way. Follow him. And yet, when Jesus turns and looks behind him, what does he see – you?

We do not have to do what Jesus did. God was at work in him, doing for us what we cannot do for ourselves. But we are to follow his leadership and walk in his steps. He will help you find the way and get to where your life is supposed to go. On the way, you can help others get in step with him.

When Jesus looks out from the cross, will he see us coming over the hill tracking his trail? Or are we confidently headed to Harrisburg?

HONEY

I had another birthday, and women everywhere have taken to calling me "honey". I am not sure if I have become suddenly irresistible or just doddery. (This is not a poll, please.) Actually, the women are not everywhere, just (so far) restaurant servers and telemarketers.

The restaurant servers tend to call me "Hon," probably abbreviating their feelings because they are in a hurry. But I had a telemarketer last week come right out with "honey". She was from the Japanese Sheriff's Association, or at least that's what I think she said. She sounded to me more like she was from Mississippi, but as soon as I showed interest ("What the heck is the Japanese Sheriff's Association?"), I was her honey as she sweetly explained to me that it would be awfully expensive for them to keep going unless I sent some money immediately.

How things change when people have a new name for you: *Doctor… Coach… Sweetheart… Doofus… Boss… "Mrs."* A new name alters the landscape, transforming how others regard you, what they expect of you, and how you think of yourself.

In the repercussion of Easter, we are given a new name, *Christian*. Through Christ's death and resurrection, God is redeeming us, claiming us, naming us as God's own. We become Christians who belong to Christ. The marks of Calvary are not just on Jesus' hands; we are marked as well.

What is in a name? That is well worth our meditation in the light of Easter. What's in this name, *Christian*, that will claim us? What will it bring to us and demand from us? How will it change us when we discover that the tomb is empty and an angel says to us, "Honey, he is not here; he is risen!"

EASTER

OUTSIDE THE TOMB

God was thinking outside the tomb. We call that, *Easter*. These days, "thinking outside the box" is highly valued, and creative people often encourage each other to do just that. Think outside the box. But the Creator who first invented creativity is way ahead of us. God was thinking outside the tomb.

Mary Magdalene went to Jesus' tomb out of respect, love, and sorrow. She went to the tomb where his body had been placed, where what remained of Jesus would be found, inside the tomb. She walked there thinking of him inside the tomb. It is where we all end up, where death puts us. They say only two things are certain, death and taxes, but there are ways to resist and avoid the latter. Death runs uncontested, and always wins. Those in the grave remain in the grave. That's why we call them *remains*.

Jesus would be inside the tomb. That is where religious intolerance puts us. As does the power of the empire to anyone who threatens it, and they were right that Jesus was a threat to the empire. The tomb is the destination of our hopes and fears, loves and endeavors, sooner or later. The tomb looms out there advising us to eat, drink, and be merry now, for tomorrow we die, and there is no future beyond it.

Inside the tomb: There is no need for prayer or devotion, for a Supreme Being or Higher Power, for exerting yourself to bring justice or sacrificing yourself to carry out mercy. Forgiveness is hardly necessary, and humility is foolish. Loving one another is only worthwhile if it is to your immediate benefit. Because: this world and you are not going anywhere. There is no future beyond the tomb. Death wins. Always.

And yet, on that morning we call Easter, the tomb was empty. God was thinking outside the tomb. Every morning since, God has been thinking outside the tomb. "He is alive!" challenges us with a future of hope and promise beyond the tomb.

"Christ is risen!" invites you to join him in living outside the tomb.

HIDDEN TRASH

I am told of a college (seminary?) campus of years gone by where winter-long snows provided a continual white blanket. Snow has a way of hiding things, and as the wintry days wore on it was not noticeable when something was tossed aside or thrown to the ground. Paper, bottles, a dropped pencil... also a bundle of trash, an old shoe, some rusty pipe that had been replaced, a broken bedspring, each with its own story of how it had found its way to the ground only to be forgotten or lost in the accumulating snow.

Spring thaw came. Driven quickly by the bright sun, this thaw steamed on until the old snow seemed to simply vanish. And what to wondering eyes did appear? Rubbish, everywhere. A sea of trash and litter blighted this otherwise venerable and highly respected campus. Some would laugh and others blush at the sudden revelation. They had spent the winter in academic refinement and theological reflection while the trash piled up unseen around them.

For those who live in my part of the world, it seems so timely that Easter comes hand-in-hand with spring. For it soon becomes clear that Palm Sunday snowballs tossed so playfully toward Jesus also conceal rocks from Calvary's hilltop. As Holy Week wears on, it is demonstrated how trashy our lives can be. That should be no surprise. Anyone who cares to closely observe either that campus or our own mirror reflection can recognize the truth of what lies hidden beneath the surface.

The true surprise is not our suddenly revealed trash, but that in the Easter light the trash is gone! Our inner landscape of the soul that connects us with others and stretches out to God has been cleaned up. Easter makes all things new.

We can, of course, garbage can in hand, insist on combing the grounds for the concealed debris that must be around here somewhere, intent on cleaning up our own mess. Or we can take a walk in the Easter dawn, stroll across this new landscape of God's redeeming love, and give thanks we won't have to mow around all that rubbish.

WRONG LINE

At King's Cross train station, London, many train lines converge. We stood there huffing a bit from hauling our luggage a busy block or two. Having just missed the early train, we found ourselves almost first in line at the track promising the next train to Edinburgh. That was a relief. Now there would be no pressure to find seats together for the journey.

As the hour wore on, the line grew and grew behind us, and a certain sense of satisfaction, even smugness, swelled up inside us at the thought of being practically first in this long line of people waiting for our train.

Uneasiness crept in, however, as the hour approached and no train appeared on our track.

"Delay," was the murmur up and down the line. Suddenly, a uniformed voice appeared to us announcing that our train was now on Track #6, somewhere off to the left. I don't know what happened to the British sense of order, but a mad dash ensued, recalling students swarming the field after the game-winning touchdown. In a moment, we went from first to almost last. Smugness gave way to befuddlement. Train cars quickly filled as we walked from one to another. I asked a porter where we should sit; he replied, "Somewhere else, just not here." Finally, we found seats in a car inexplicably almost empty. We soon discovered why – it was the smoking car. On the whole journey to Edinburgh, passengers looked questioningly at us, and in some cases asked us, "Why are you in this car if you don't smoke?"

Good question. Answer: because we were at the front of the wrong line.

Easter must have felt something like that. It still does, doesn't it? We get in line right behind Pilate, Herod, the chief priests, and most of the disciples, satisfied that while the Good Friday events were tragic, we at least know where we stand and where we will sit when the train comes. Then Easter startles and unnerves with the uniformed angel's announcement that we are on the wrong track, this tomb is empty, the train we seek is not here. What a mad dash of soldiers reporting to Pilate, priests falling all over themselves, and disciples scurrying around not knowing what to make of it.

I confess to a certain comfort at the world being the way it is. Even with all the violence, hunger, suffering, and trouble lined up behind me, I am familiar with how it goes and know my place in this line-up. What a shock, then, to have Easter inform me, this year once again, that I am in the wrong line, standing behind the wrong leader, in a line that is not in fact going anywhere, and whose promises will not come true. What am I to think when this world to which I am accustomed starts to disintegrate, as people scramble to get on track with the Risen Christ?

That's Easter – shaking up the world around me, offering a ride in Christ to a new world and new life, leaving me standing alone by an empty track if I refuse to move.

SPIDER

I was driving down the road, quite oblivious to anything unusual about to happen, when suddenly a fair-sized spider dropped down from the sun visor on its homemade rope and dangled between my face and the windshield. This was so unusual that I restrained the first impulse to brush it out of the way.

The spider did make it difficult to drive, bobbing and swaying just inches in front of my eyes, demanding my immediate, close-up attention while I tried to keep my driving focus on the more distant landscape. It was weird, that in-my-face spider appearing huge against the countryside, with the wide world into which my car was rushing now seeming small and distant, but with a distinct, spider-ish cast to it. My perspective had changed.

I think about Easter, its celebration once again at hand. Most unexpectedly, altogether astoundingly, soon after the death of Jesus and his entombment, while his disciples are driving down the road of their grief and his enemies are headed back home in relief, Jesus appears again right before their eyes. Resurrection, so close and immediate, as Thomas found out, they could reach out and touch it.[22]

Now disciples see the world with this resurrected Christ in the forefront of their vision. Everything looks different. Even those who deny it, who refuse to believe there is anything dangling in front of their face, find that the world no longer looks quite the same. Christ is risen.

For some reason, I could not automatically brush aside the spider. Easter is now about as common to us as spiders, with its church celebrations and home rituals. What if you did not brush it aside this

---

[22] John 20:19-31

year (after the appropriate time of candy baskets and loud hymns), but kept Easter right in front of you as you look at your world? What if you just kept on looking at life before you through the perspective of the Easter Gospel, with Christ's resurrection power and promise dangling in your face, changing your perspective, changing everything?

May you journey on into a landscape that looks Christ-ish, christened, blessed with grace and hope.

PENTECOST

CAR FIRE

Normally, our neighborhood considers ducks waddling across the street to be an event of note. This explains our immediate interest when a neighbor's car late one evening suddenly burst into flames in the driveway. Folks in various evening attire gathered on surrounding lawns to see this thing which had come to pass. Others came from afar, having seen the flame in the east, and cruised by in homage.

This was exciting. No one could explain the fire nor from whence it came. The car had not been driven recently. But suddenly it was aflame, consumed by mystery. It was a wonder to us as it pulled us from our sleepy sofas and nighttime routines, igniting our imagination.

At the first Pentecost, there was also fire reported. Followers of Jesus, believers in his resurrection, were suddenly on fire with the Spirit of God. They had a fire burning in them that was hard to explain, but others could look at them and see it. This fire from God brought people running in bathrobes and slippers, just as they were, and then standing there together like a Nativity scene, in amazement at what God had made of them, this new nativity which God had brought forth – the Church.

Firefighters soon came, angels of mercy dressed like Herod's army. Good thing, too, lest the sparks carry. In short order they had doused the flames. How quickly a raging fire becomes a charred vehicle for the insurance adjustor. How quickly the flames within us are cooled by our spiritual thermostat. Before the smoke had cleared, we were back in our respective homes, staring numbly at the television.

But for the moment that evening, we awoke to a mysterious power, wonderfully dangerous, never far below life's surface, ready to inexplicably burst forth and draw us all to it, a fire that is more than flame, the Holy Spirit of the Living God.

BED HOG

A Sunday School project used *Jesus dolls*. Similar to checking out a book from the library, a child could take home a Jesus doll for a week at a time. Children were encouraged to do this. The teaching goal was the idea of having Jesus with you. Hopefully, the children would begin to understand about God being present in our lives. What a friend we have in Jesus.

One girl, however, unhappily returned her Jesus doll. She had a complaint. She had taken the doll to bed with her, and she reported, "Jesus hogged the whole bed!"[23]

Exactly. Many an adult has had the same experience. Jesus somehow finds us, through our parents, the influence of friends, an act of mercy, or some life-rattling event. Jesus finds us, and we begin to find in Jesus truth and meaning. There is something about Jesus, crucified and risen, that draws us to him. Our lives become interwoven with what he reveals to us of God and how he guides us. Next thing we know, he is hogging the whole bed! When we involve Jesus with our lives, he likes to hog the whole thing – all our heart, all of our mind, and all our spirit.

When on Pentecost the Spirit of God came to the first disciples, it took over their lives. The Holy Spirit filled the room. It was like a mighty wind overwhelming them, taking them where they would not otherwise have gone. God's Spirit was a fire consuming them, burning onto their hearts a new identity. This Pentecost Spirit pushed and stretched and sprawled until they were shoved out of their old lives, and rolled into the church.

---

[23] Thanks to my colleague, Rev. Michael Moore, who told me this story.

When the Spirit of God comes, it ensures that Jesus will from now on hog your whole life.

LEADERSHIP

Some years ago I wrote in the *personal statement* in my resume that "pastors can do a lot more harm than good." This seemed to amuse search committees and strike a knowing chord as they eyed me skeptically. What I meant was that single-handedly pastors can not do much good because that takes a whole church working together. But single-handedly a pastor can certainly throw a wrench in the works.

I have been musing lately on the vital importance of leadership, not only that of clergy but also leadership from the laity. Sometimes leaders confuse God's will with their own certainties, and exchange listening for God's direction with getting the job done. This has left the church landscape too often littered with the debris of hurts and division and missed opportunities.

Add to this the wider church leadership of conference ministers, denominational presidents, and bishops (if you have them) who have a heck of a hard job in such times as these, sometimes excelling as true servants and sometimes making a mess of it.

All of which leads me to suggest that if you have ever wondered about that Pentecost business in Acts chapter 2, with the strange story of the arrival of the Holy Spirit which then pulled the disciples together into a church, you can see the evidence all around still today. Just look at the church and the way we do things. Just look at some of its leadership. The Spirit of God *must be in this*, must be at work in the church, or it would not last out the week.

Pentecost reminds that the church belongs to God. That is very Good News.

EXPECTING THE SPIRIT

When we worshiped with a church in Costa Rica, they seemed to be expecting the Holy Spirit. This was the congregation with whom we partnered in the construction of a house for a young family. At the end of the week we worshiped with them. Their worship style and order were predictably different. What struck me however was a sense that I was in the company of people who expected the Spirit of God to show up. People who wanted that to happen that very day. As if it would be a good thing.

"Spirit of the living God, fall afresh on me," we sing here at home. It sounds like a blessing. Spirit of God: sun-kiss my days, calm my nights, whisper an encouraging word, open a window, provide an insight, prompt a decision, gently lead me. This is the Spirit I find myself summoning and expecting. A Spirit of God that will correct, enhance or perhaps refocus my life without substantial reconstruction.

I recite with you the scripture, "Come, Holy Spirit, come," hoping for at best a blessing. Anything more would be a surprise. Anything more and I would have some conditions. Were the Spirit to come like a mighty wind through my life or like fire in my bones, I would want to schedule it. "Come, Spirit, but not until Tuesday." Not until after summer vacation which is pre-paid. Not until I am ready.

Were the Spirit to come in a way that turns my life upside down, I might want to negotiate. "Come, Holy Spirit, but could we spread out the full impact over the next 12 months?" There is so much in my life right now to which I want to cling. A tune-up was more what I had in mind.

The Holy Spirit in the *Acts of the Apostles* is life changing when it comes. This may be why it seems so alien, so hard to embrace, why we speak of it so tentatively. I am not sure that I am ready for my life to be transformed.

That congregation in Costa Rica was ready. When they said, "Come, Holy Spirit," it sure sounded like they meant now. Today would be fine. They were ready for a transformation. They were ready for a world not so sharply divided between rich and poor. They were ready not to be poor, for suffering to be gone, for less struggling, for a new future. They were ready for changed lives. And they expected it. They expected the Spirit of God to come. Maybe today.

When you join to say, "Come, Holy Spirit, come," or simply utter, "Please, God, help!" what do you mean? What do you expect?

ALL SAINTS

REMEMBERING

In late autumn, around what is widely called All Saints Day, we remember those church members who have died in the past twelve months, while recalling many others who have gone before them. The *saints* we call them, not because of moral virtue, though that may be true, but "saints" as ordinary people who have sought to live by faith in Jesus Christ. At worship, we light candles for these saints who have now died in faith, and we believe died into the everlasting love of God.

This ceremony of remembering is a sobering time for me. People who were so much part of my daily life and who loomed so large on my landscape are suddenly removed. Their memory and influence may carry on, but they are gone. Now you see them, now you don't. Death may bring terrible, lingering grief and loss to loved ones. For the most part, however, the world goes on. The funeral is held, ham sandwiches and Jello salad are consumed, and the next day we continue with the business of living. That is the way it must be.

But it is sobering. Death is abrupt. The mark you were making on the world soon gets painted over. Life is fragile. Remembering the saints reminds me how wonderful this gift of life is ... and how fleeting. I find this ritual of honoring the everyday saints to be humbling.

I also find it uplifting. Somehow it makes me understand that this all belongs on a bigger stage. I see more clearly that our lives are part of a greater drama. We are not alone. The God who created us continues to be active. The God who imagines the future keeps that vision alive. "Resurrection, life out of death?" yes, but more: vindication, blessing, all that was good and holy about someone's life on earth being used by God as raw material for a new heaven and new earth ... and at last, reason to hope. At the end of life is God, who is also the beginning.

There is more going on with my life than I can know. I am not alone here. As the song about saints tells it, *"Thou wast their rock, their fortress, and their might, thou Lord their captain in the well-fought fight, thou in the darkness drear, their one true light."* And finally: *"And when the strife is fierce, the warfare long, steals on the ear the distant triumph song, and hearts are brave again and arms are strong."*[24]

---

[24] "For All the Saints" William Walsham How

THANKSGIVING

HAWK TOWER

Walking the path to the Hawk Tower, I wonder: would today bring hundreds... thousands... the rare and elusive? For years I have heard about Holiday Beach, a conservation area on the Ontario shore of Lake Erie. This is one of the great spots to observe a phenomenon of nature, the annual hawk migration. For a few weeks in autumn countless hawks wing their way southward. As they come to Lake Erie, they turn westward to skirt the lake before continuing south. That brings them right over Holiday Beach and the Hawk Tower where I am headed.

For years I have been trying to make this trip. Now finally I am here and at the right time, late September. The weather is decent. The wind comes from the right direction, aiding the birds in their flight, encouraging them to come my way. Tens of thousands of broad-winged hawks have recently passed through, departing Canada in swirling kettles overhead. Would a few hundred slowpokes soar by today? Will a hungry and powerful peregrine swoop upon a duck in the marsh around me? Will there be multiple merlins migrating today, enough to help me learn to identify them from kestrels at a distance? And will there (my great hope for the day) be an unlikely but possible goshawk, a hawk I have never seen but that does pass this way?

I mostly have the Hawk Tower to myself, except for the official spotter who is assigned to count and record the migrating hawks. Good – he can help me identify the hard ones. Ok, here we go: First hour, no hawks yet. Second hour, one sharp-shinned... write that down. Third hour, none; ducks, yes, and a local bald eagle, but that's all. Time for lunch. Afternoon, there are still no migrating hawks. Why not, what's keeping them back? Some days are like that. At mid-afternoon, the spotter gives up and heads for home. He calls it his second worst day ever at this (the worst was in a sleet storm). The next day I go back to the hawk tower, ever hopeful... hundreds today, surely dozens? No spotter bothers to show up. For good reason, I realize, as I pace around waiting and watching, preaching a couple of sermons you would not want to hear. In the end, I double yesterday's count. Two. I could have done as well from my backyard at home.

Yet, as I wait on that tower, I begin to be aware of the blue jays. There are a lot of blue jays today. Blue jays in bunches overhead, heading west and south. I see blue jays by the dozens flying by at eye level. And blue jays stopping to rest in trees around me. Just how many are there? Until the hawks come, I count blue jays. In a 30 minute period, I see 3,000. Three thousand, now that I am paying attention. It occurs to me that all through yesterday and today there have been blue jays migrating through, six thousand an hour! But I mostly missed them, not looking for them. Coming for the hawk migration, I almost missed altogether the real show.

Looking for the right thing is ever the challenge of **thanksgiving**. Focusing not on what we expect God to provide, but appreciating the wonder that presents itself. Instead of the blessing predicted, marvel at the blessing that comes.

In the absence of hawks, be thankful for blue jays.

CPSIA information can be obtained at www.ICGtesting.com
Printed in the USA
LVOW10s1425151115

462654LV00001B/120/P

9 781681 110639